I0511214

A Complete Catalogue
of
Mural Paintings

by
Timothy Plant

94 Milton Rd, Belvedere, Kent, DA17 5BA
www.timanaplant.com   timanaplant@yahoo.co.uk

© Timothy Plant 2017

PREFACE

Painting murals is not just a pleasant pastime. It is an art form about as old as humanity itself. For the past 32,000 years, the artists who painted on walls have often been leading innovators in the pictorial arts. After the grand epoch of patronage in Italy, the art of mural painting went into decline. Now it seems to have come back. Indeed, it could be said that the art of mural painting is enjoying a vogue. It has done so before - at different times and places, in different cultures, for different reasons - ever since the cavemen first decided to paint images of beasts on their cave walls. In fact, because of the way it developed in their hands, the painting of murals can probably be counted as the first truly creative activity of mankind.

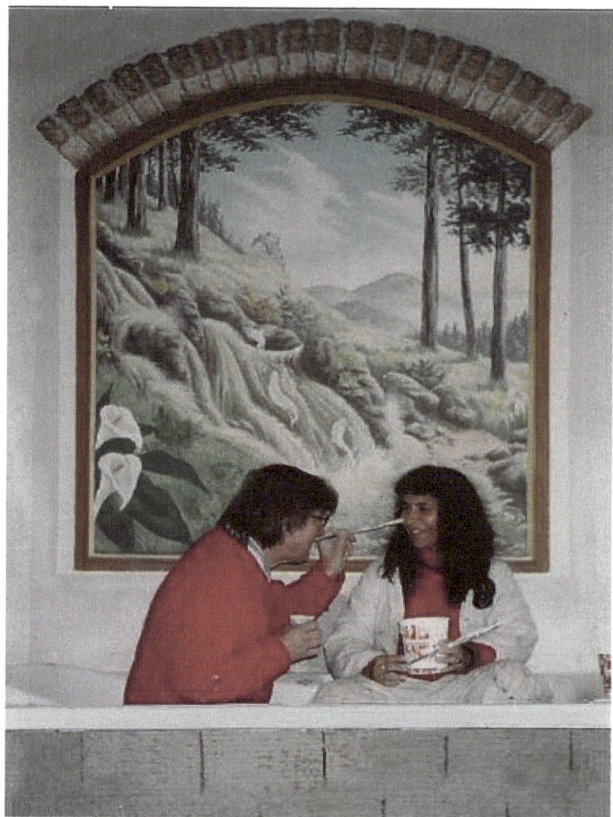

The Finishing Touch

Ana Maria Plant has been my art and business partner since our wedding in 1993. Without her help many of the works in this catalogue would probably not have happened.

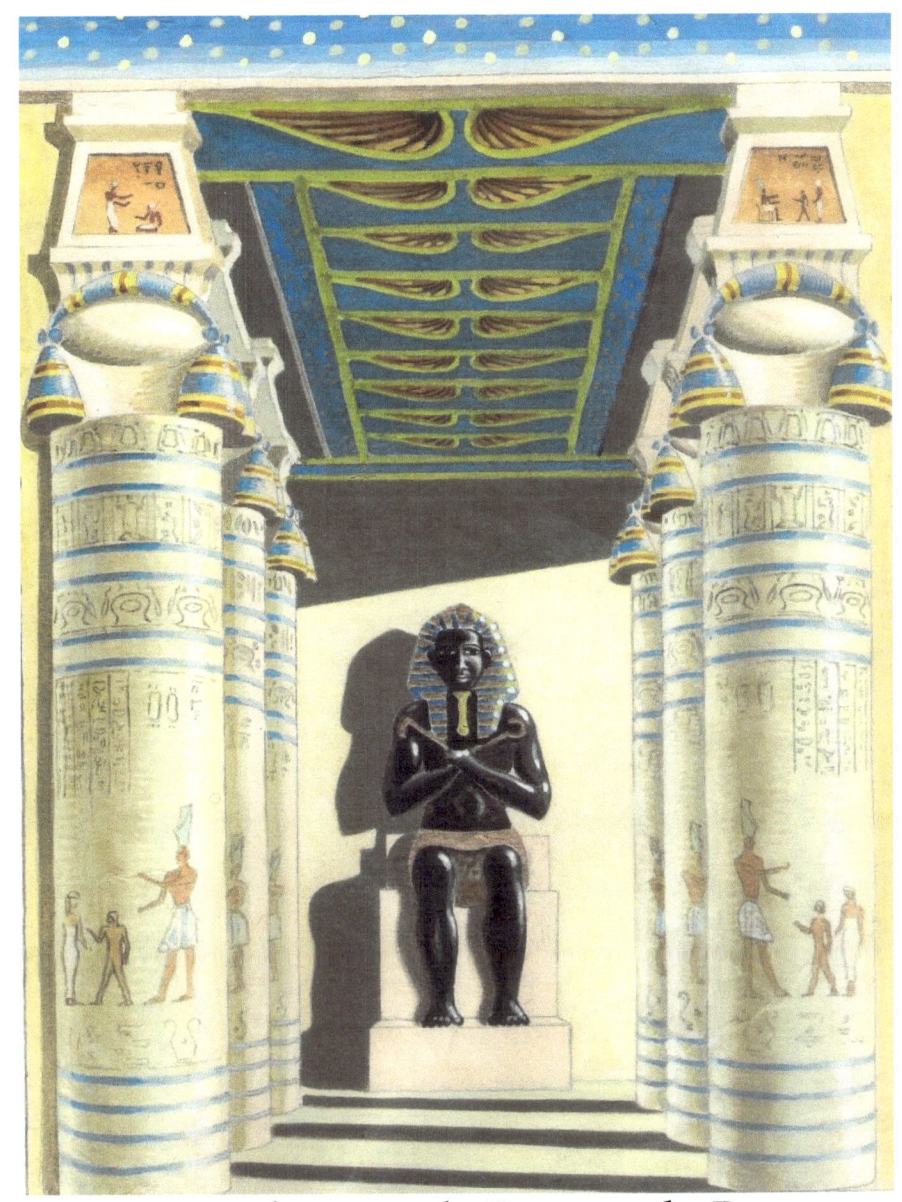

Design for a mural – Ramasses by Day

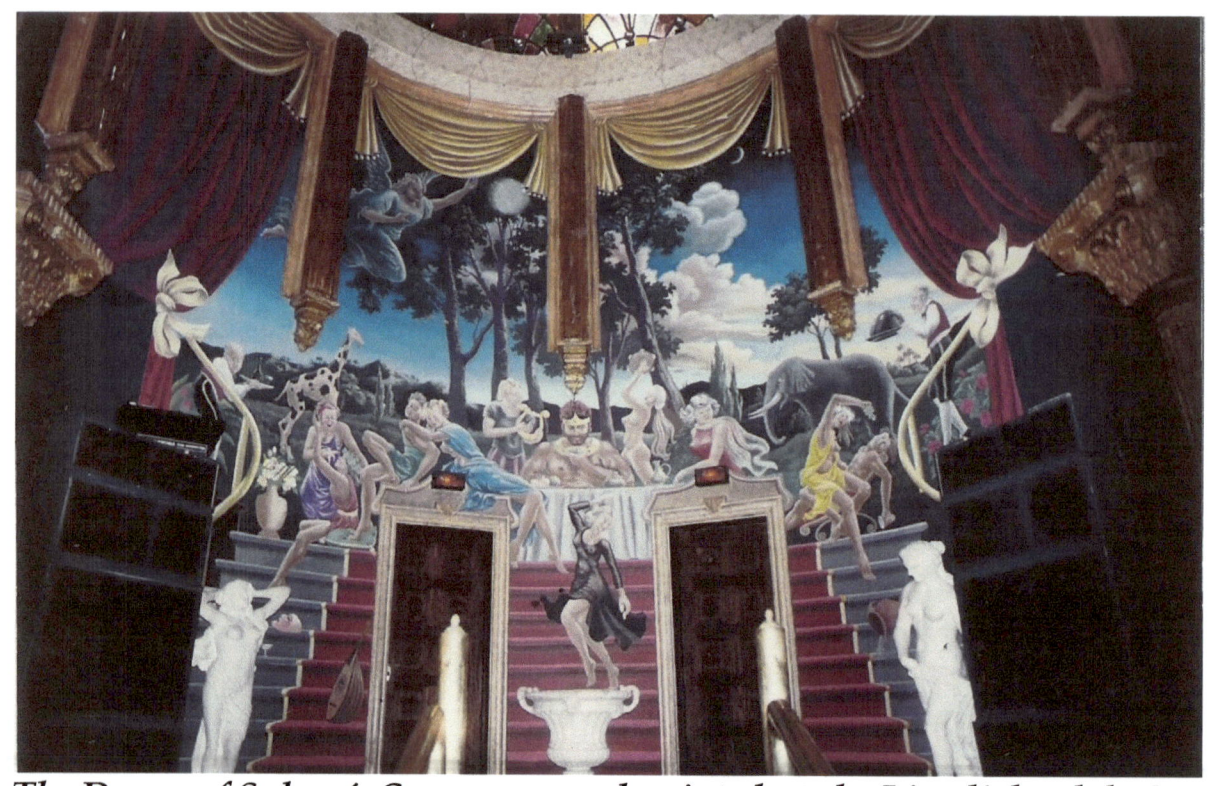

The Dance of Salomé. Concave mural painted at the Limelight club, São Paulo, Brazil. 6x9m. The waiter on the top right of the painting is carrying a silver salver with a cover. Under the cover is John the Baptist's head. The owner of the nightclub thought it a little gruesome for his patrons, so he asked us to cover it up like that. If you rubbed off the top layer of paint, however, the head would surely be there.

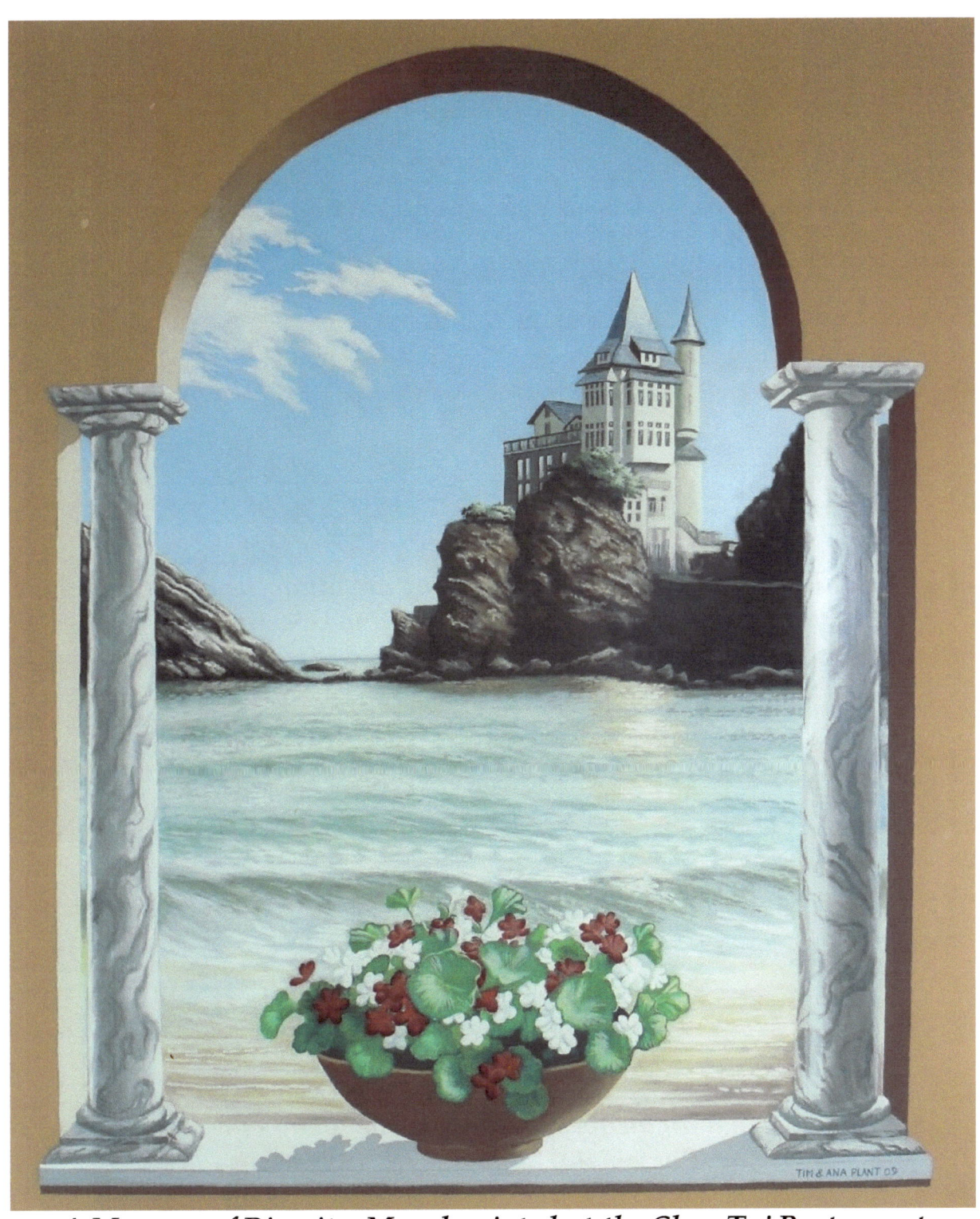

A Memory of Biarritz. Mural painted at the Chez-Toi Restaurant in Florianópolis, Brazil.

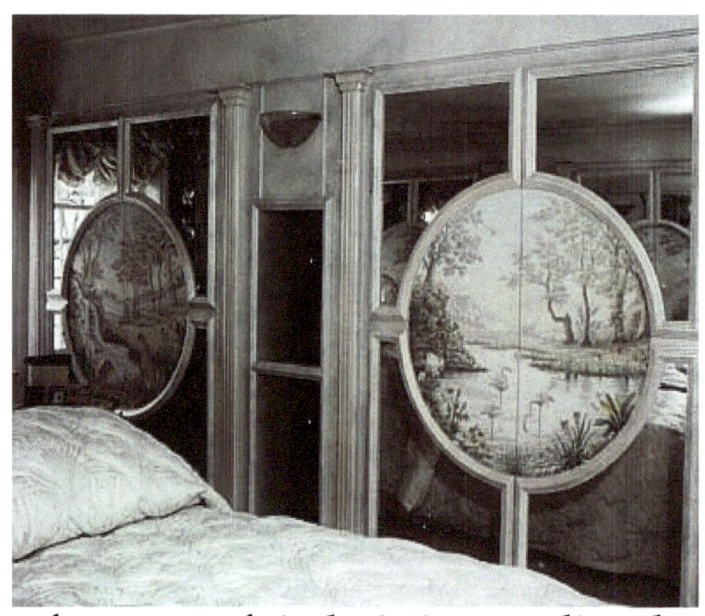

Two medallions from a set of six depicting arcadian themes, painted on the wardrobes of a London bedroom, UK. 1m each.

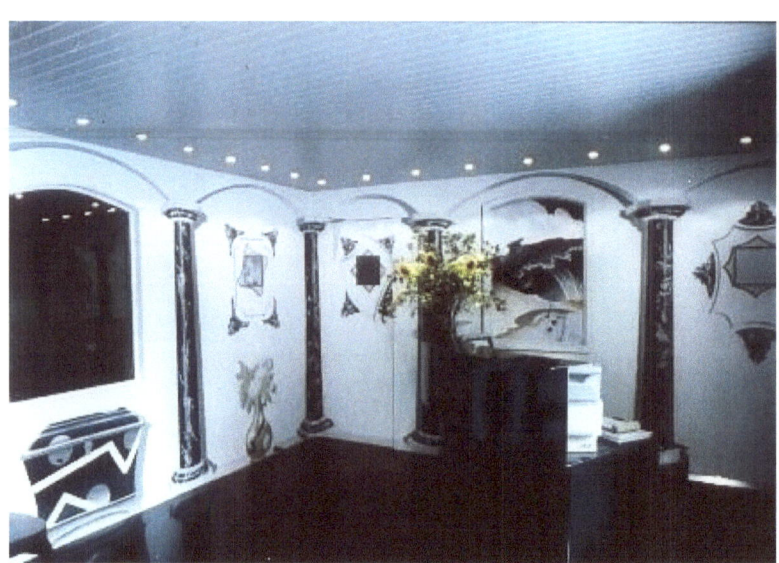

Art deco theme with alcoves, painted in the lobby of a design firm, Portobello, London, UK. 12x2m

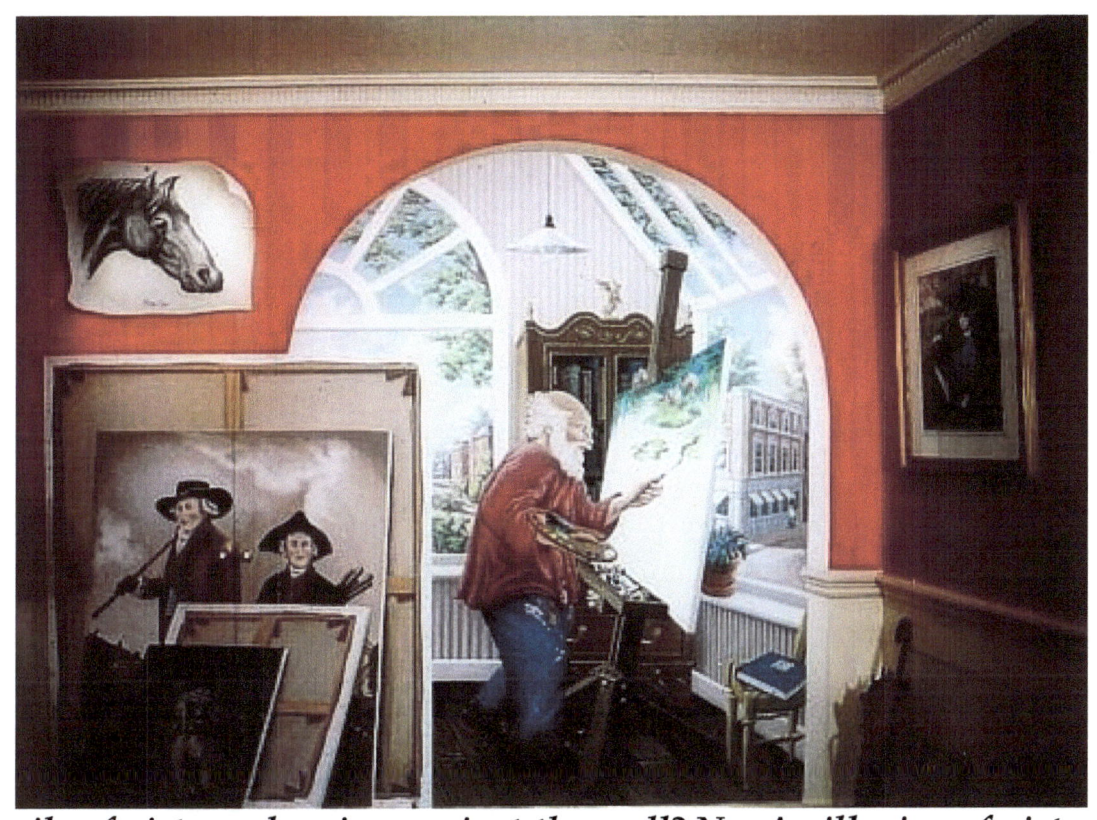

A pile of pictures leaning against the wall? No. An illusion of pictures painted on two cupboard doors. And what about that clever forger painting a Monet in the next room? Don't worry, it's just a painting on a flat wall, like the horse.

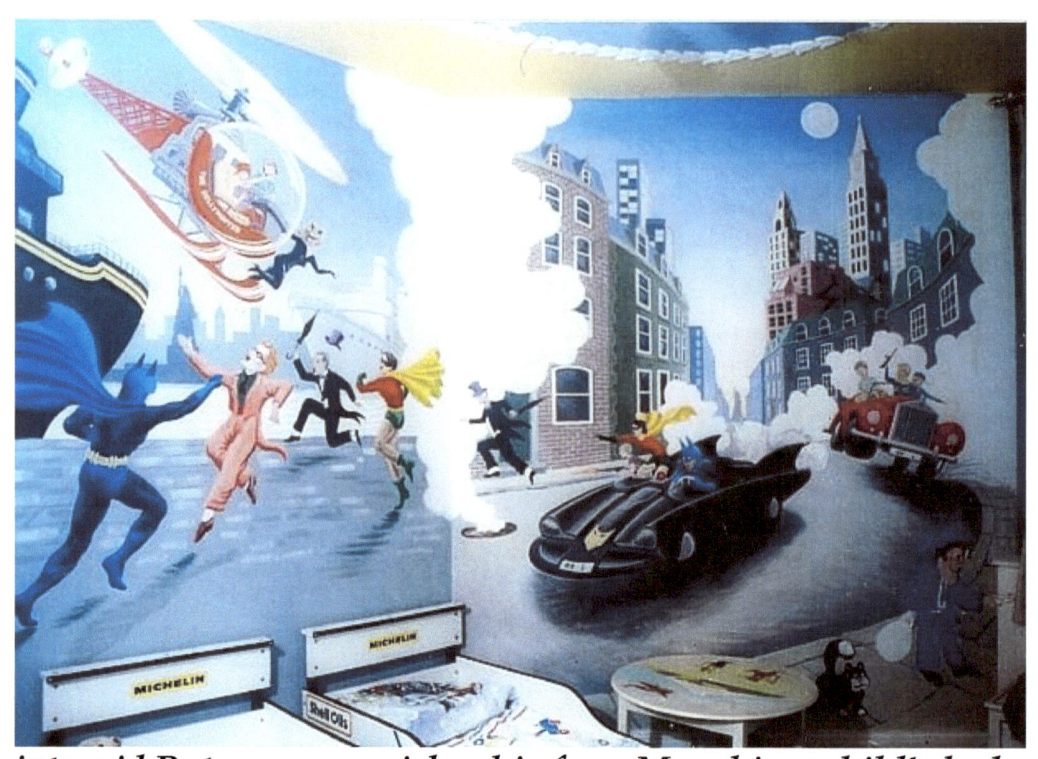

The intrepid Batman vanquishes his foes. Mural in a child's bedroom. London UK. 5x2.5m

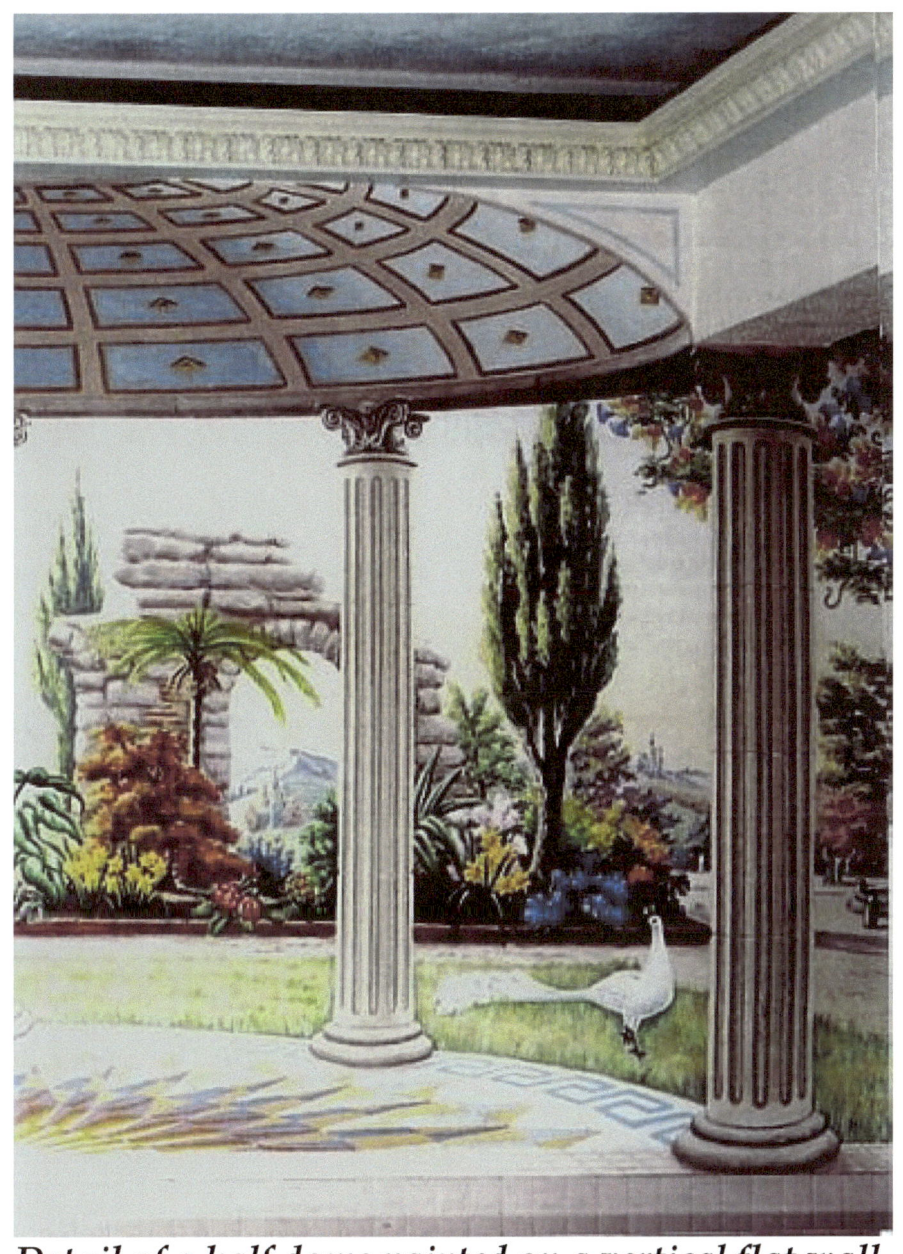

Detail of a half dome painted on a vertical flat wall.

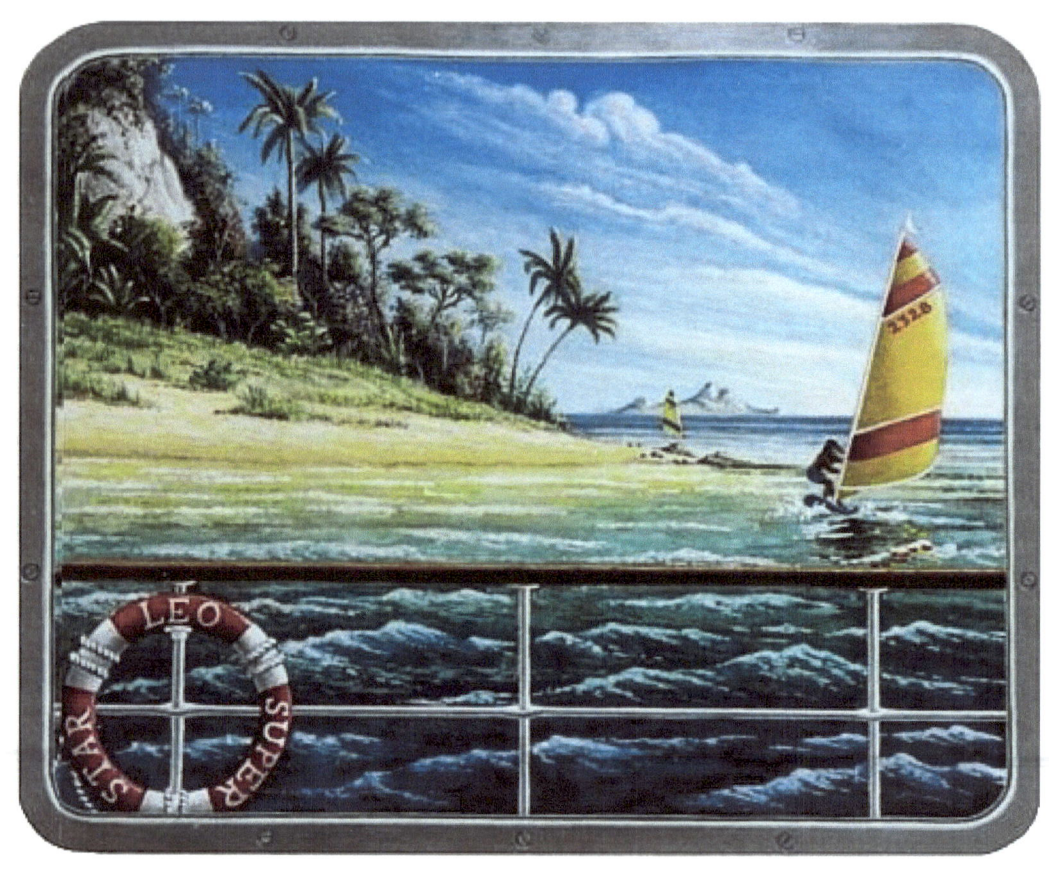

One of a series of portholes painted for cabins on the Super Star Line.
1.25x1m

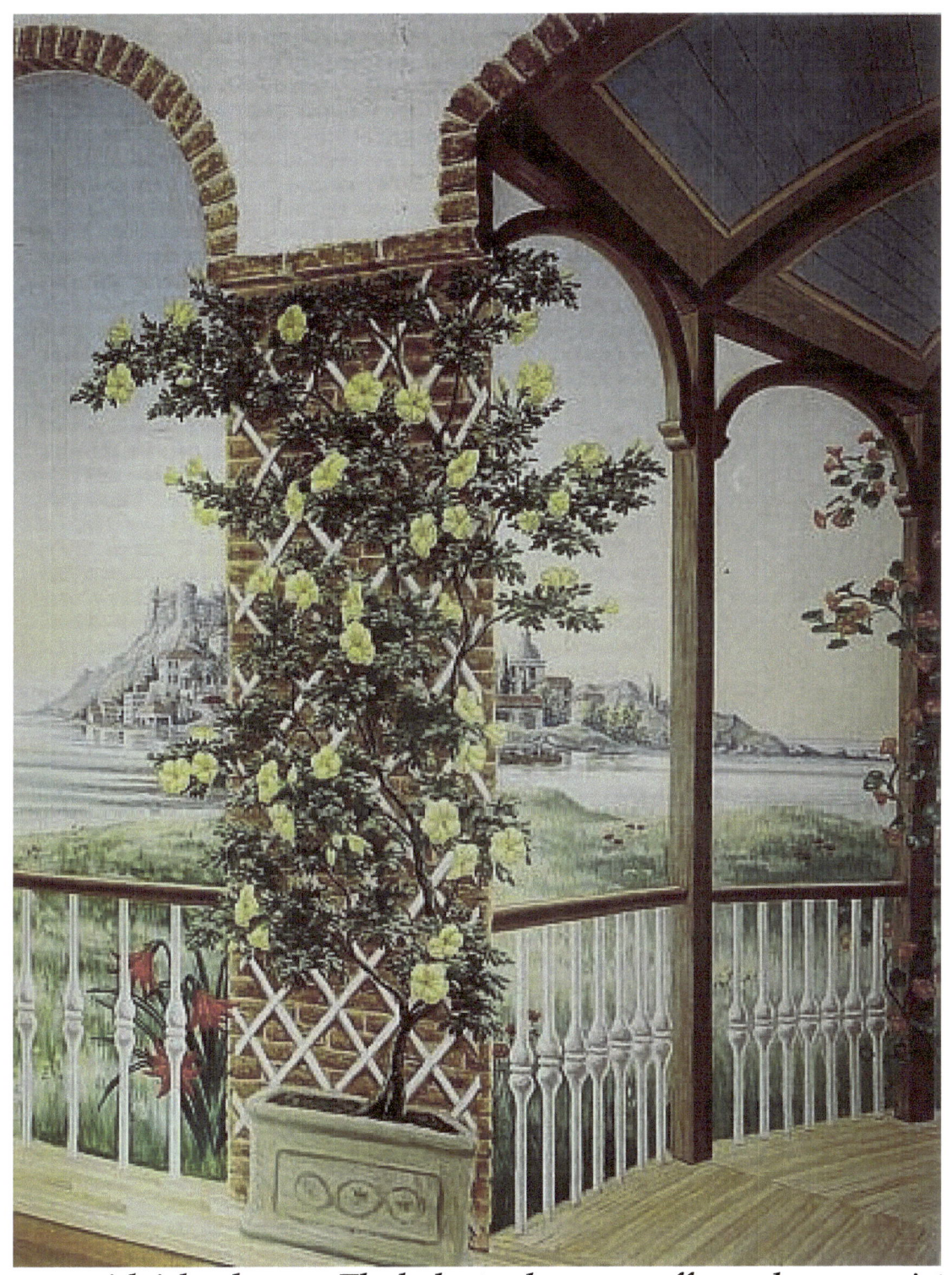

Terrace with island scene. The balustrade curves off round a non-existent corner. Painted in a sports room, London, England. 6x3.5m

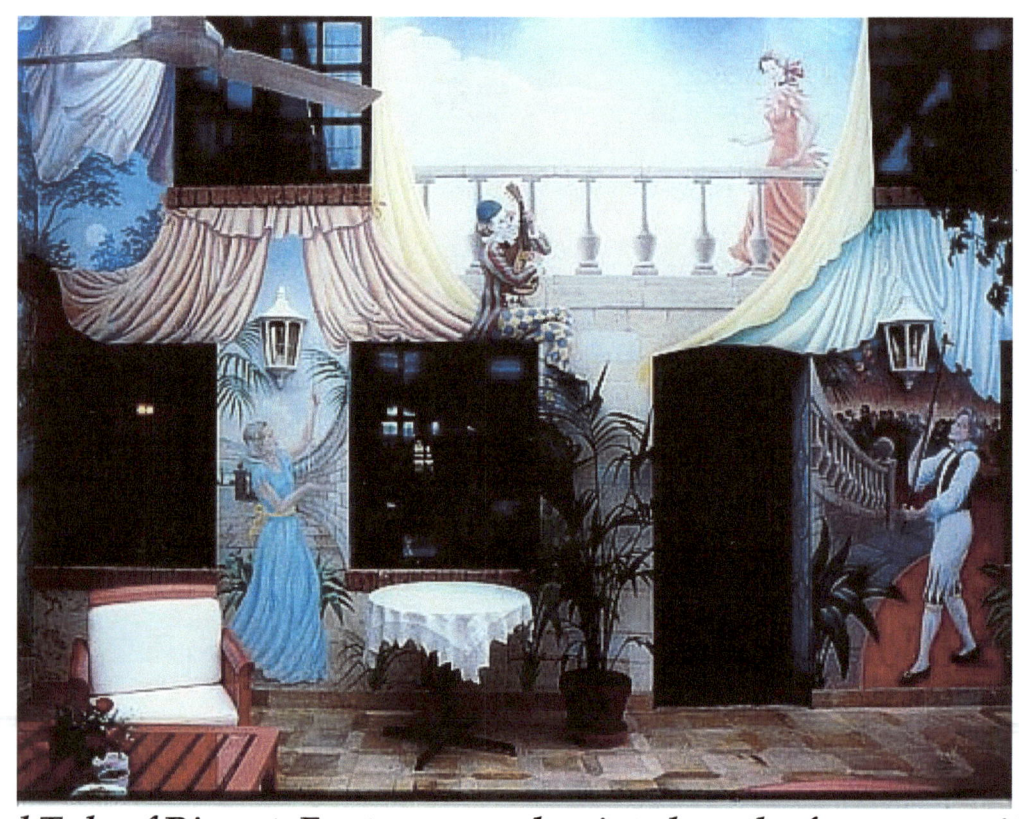

The Sad Tale of Pierrot. Fantasy mural painted on the former outside wall of an old inn, now a conservatory and restaurant. Waterhouses, England. 8x5m

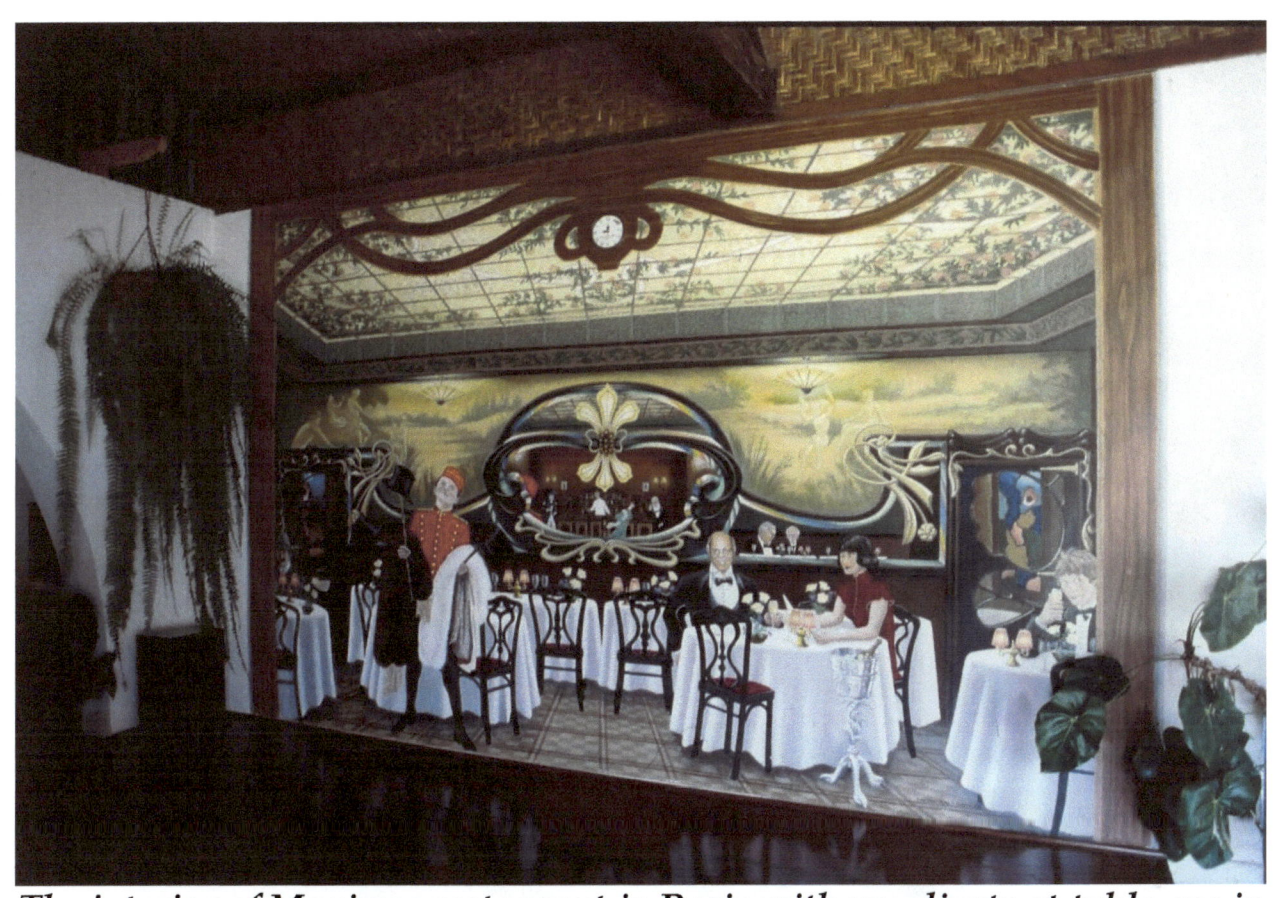

The interior of Maximes restaurant in Paris with my clients at table, me in the right-hand corner, Santos Dumont on the left, Dom Pedro II and Napoleon reflected in the mirror, plus a typical Maximes bellboy collecting hats and sticks. Painted in the ballroom of a Brazilian plantation house.
4x3m

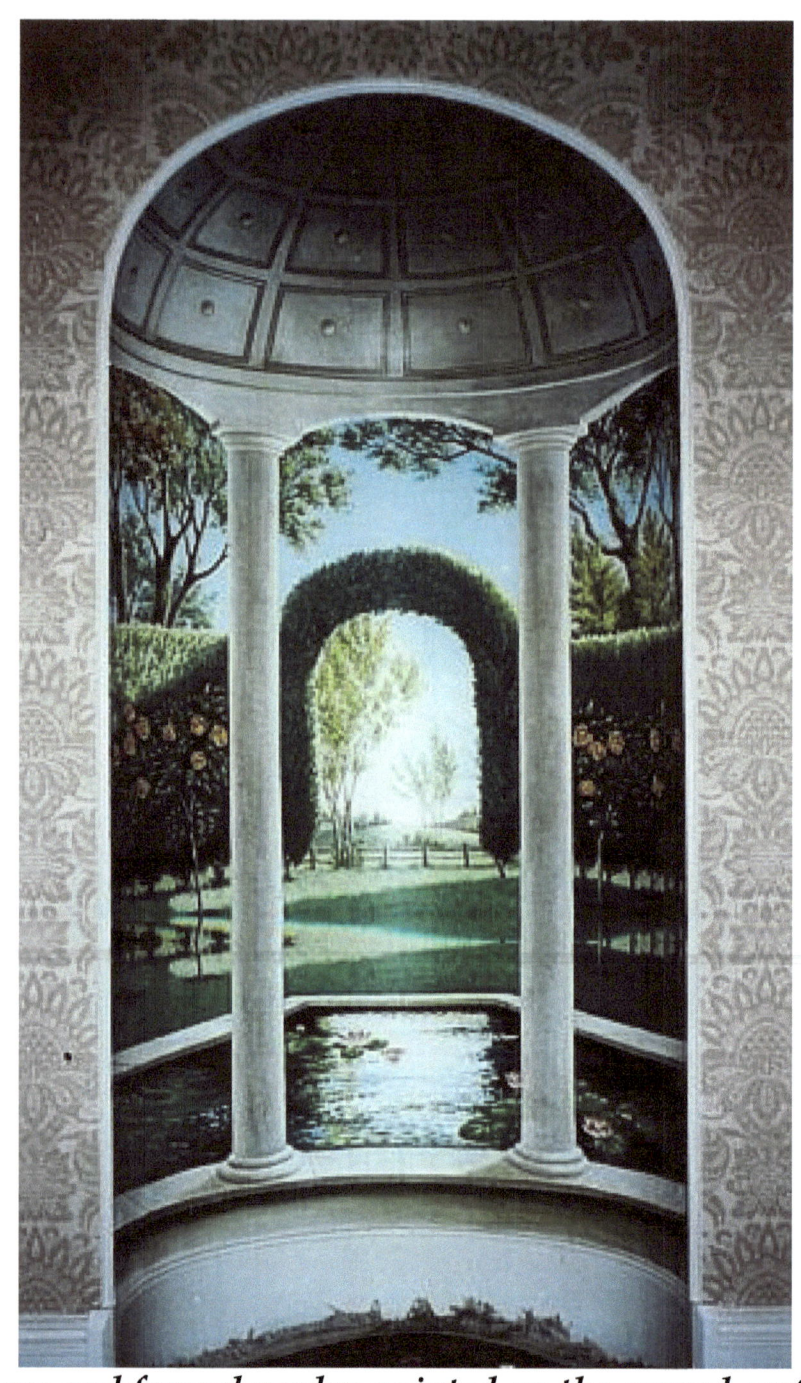

Dome and formal garden painted on the curved surface
of an alcove in the front hall, Brighton, England. 2.5x1.5m

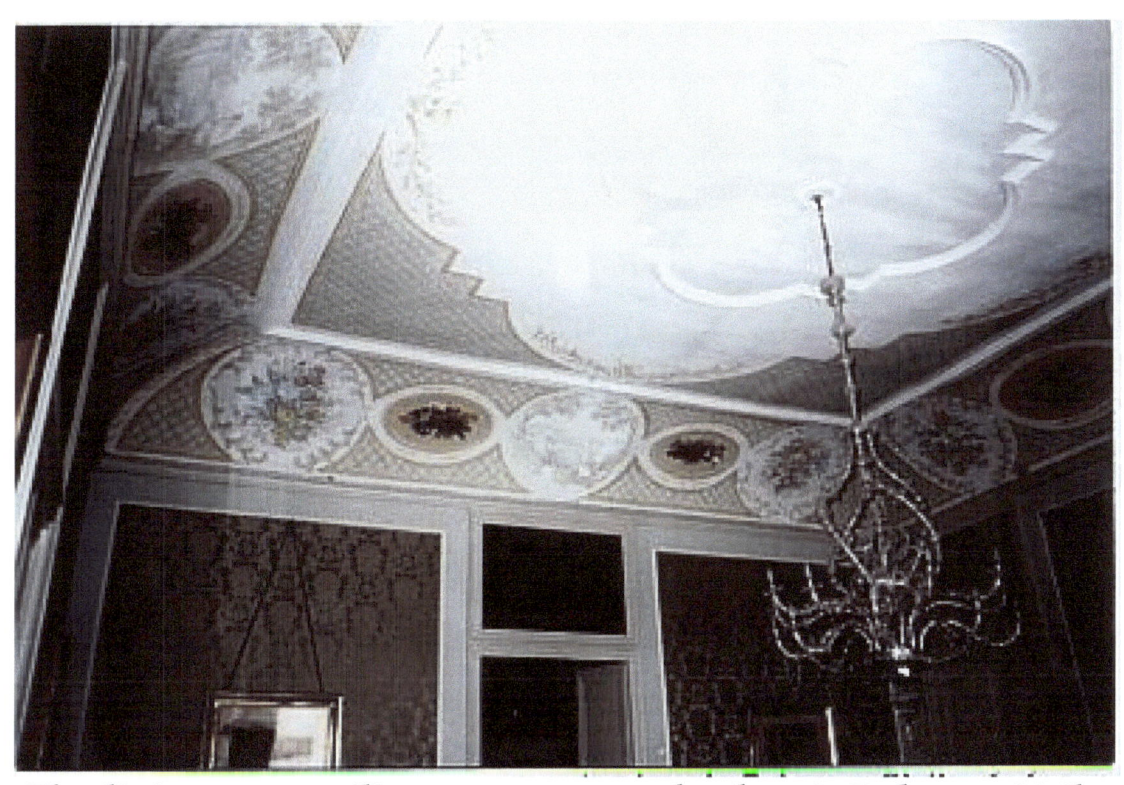

The dining-room ceiling at an ancestral palace in Palermo, Sicily,
painted in the traditional style. 7x7m

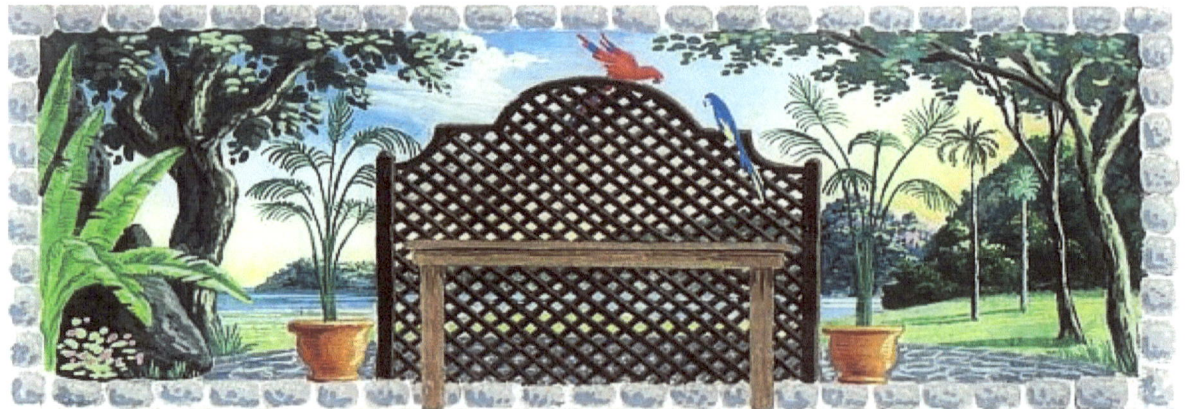

Design 1 for a mural at a beach house in Brazil.

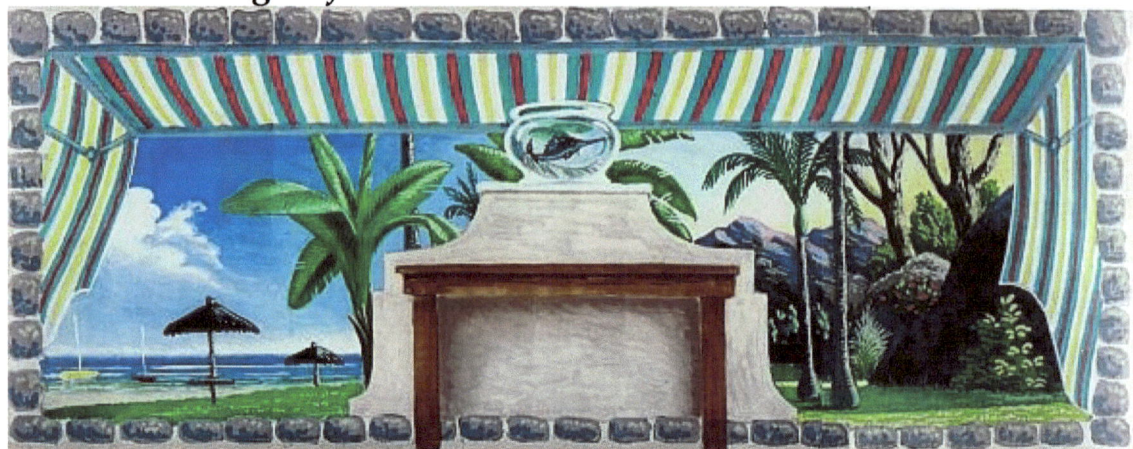

Design 2 for a mural at a beach house in Brazil.

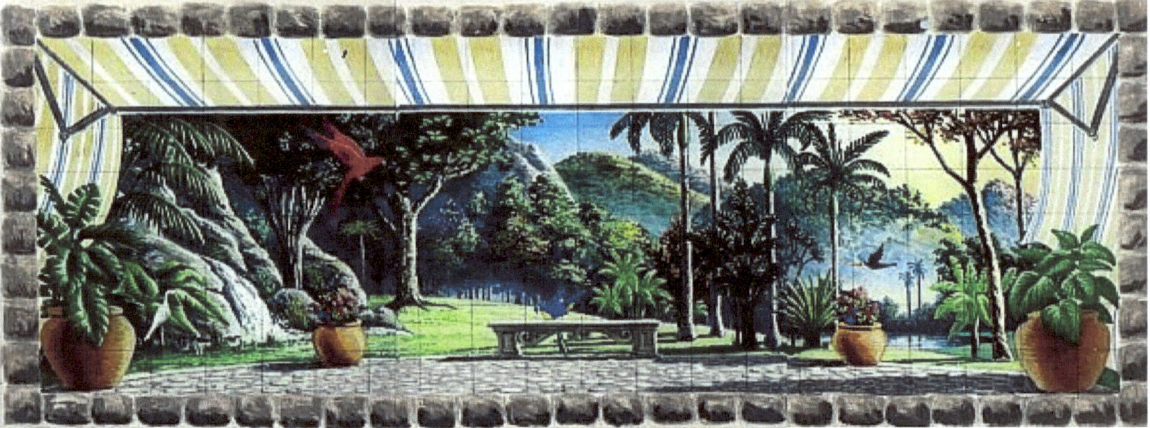

Design 3 for a mural at a beach house in Brazil. This drawing was accepted by the client and was used as the scale drawing. See the grid drawn in pencil.

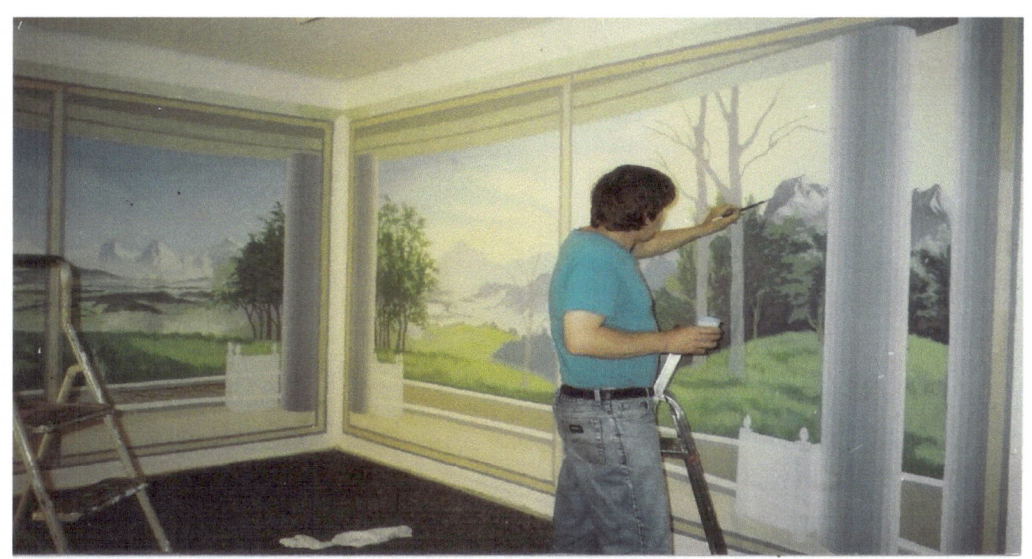

Work in progress on the Swiss mural.

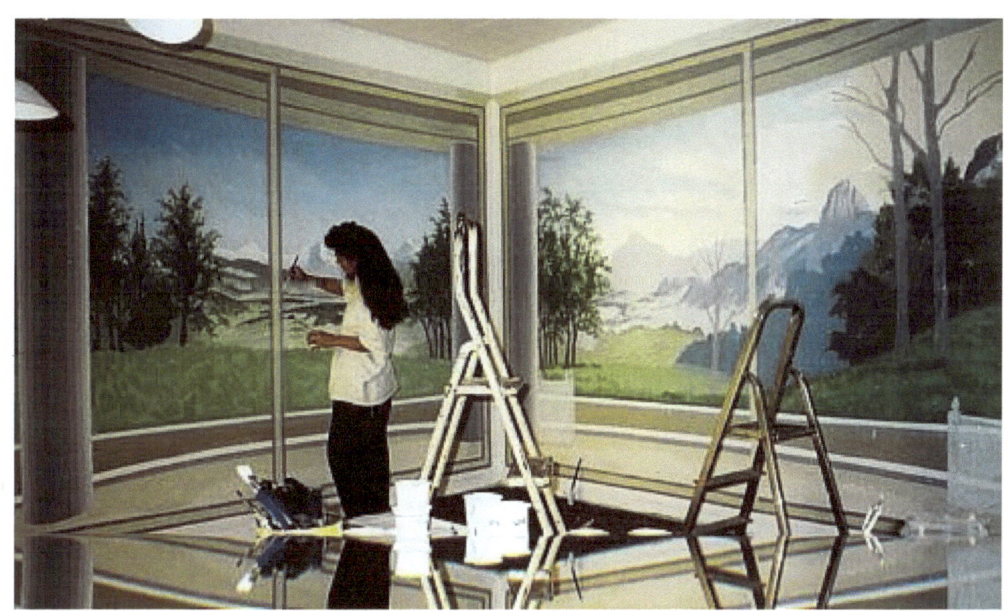

Work in progress on a scene of the Bernese Alps with windows, terrace and fountains, painted in an underground restaurant close to Interlaken, Switzerland. 10x3m

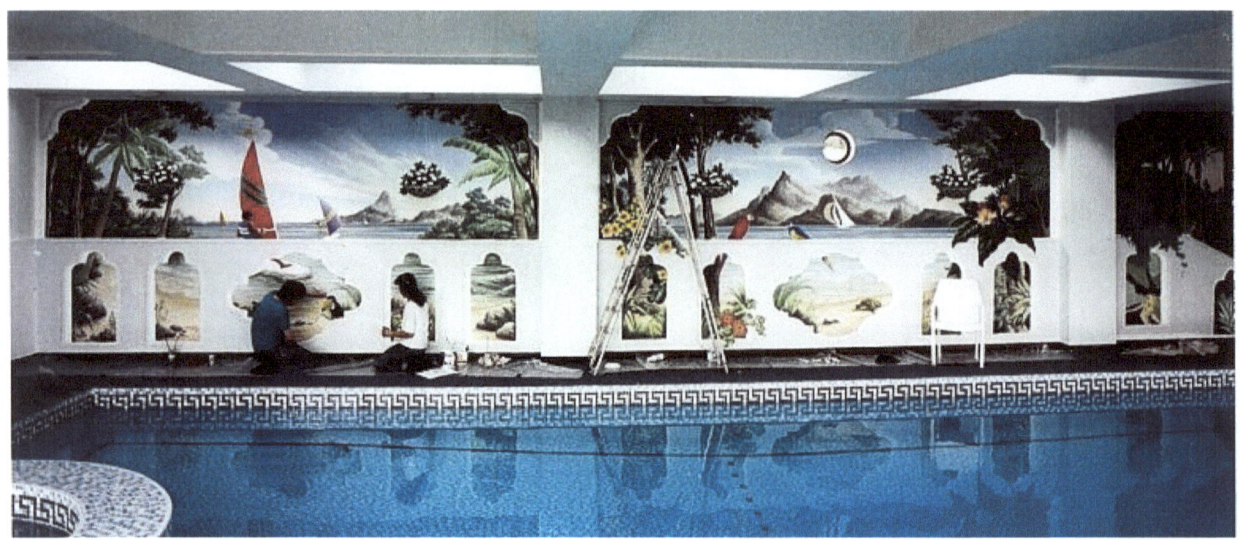

Panoramic seascape with existing structural features transformed into a colonnade and a low wall, painted beside the indoor pool at a country house near Maidstone, England. 12x3m

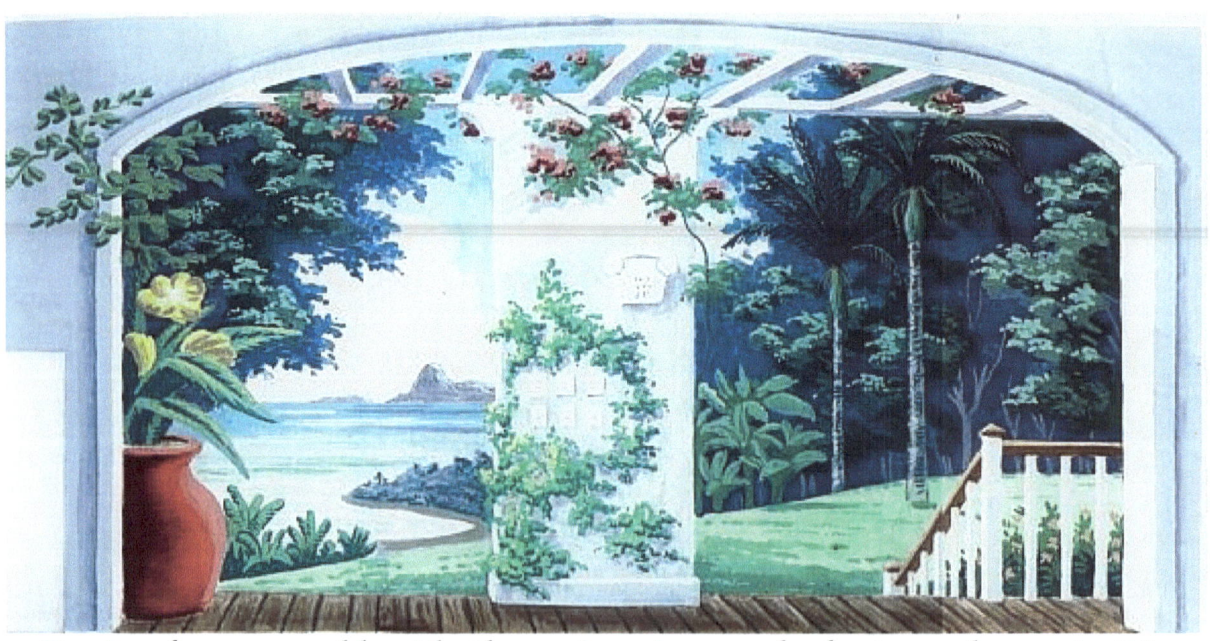

Design for a mural beside the swimming pool of a town house in São Paulo, Brazil (column included to accommodate phone and switches).

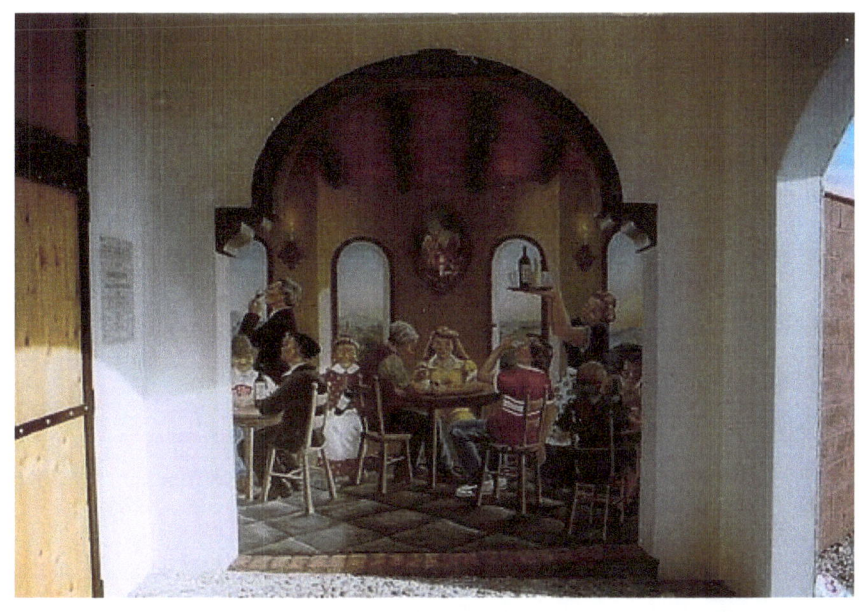

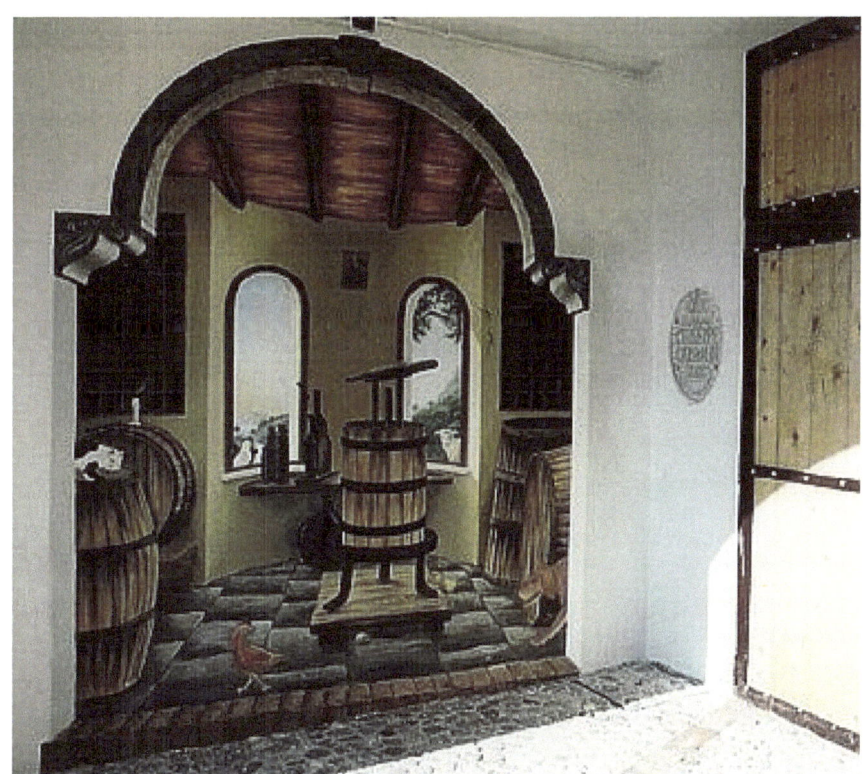

'La Festa di San Martino', when the first wine is tasted, and 'La Festa di San Francesco', when birds and animals occupy the wine press after hours

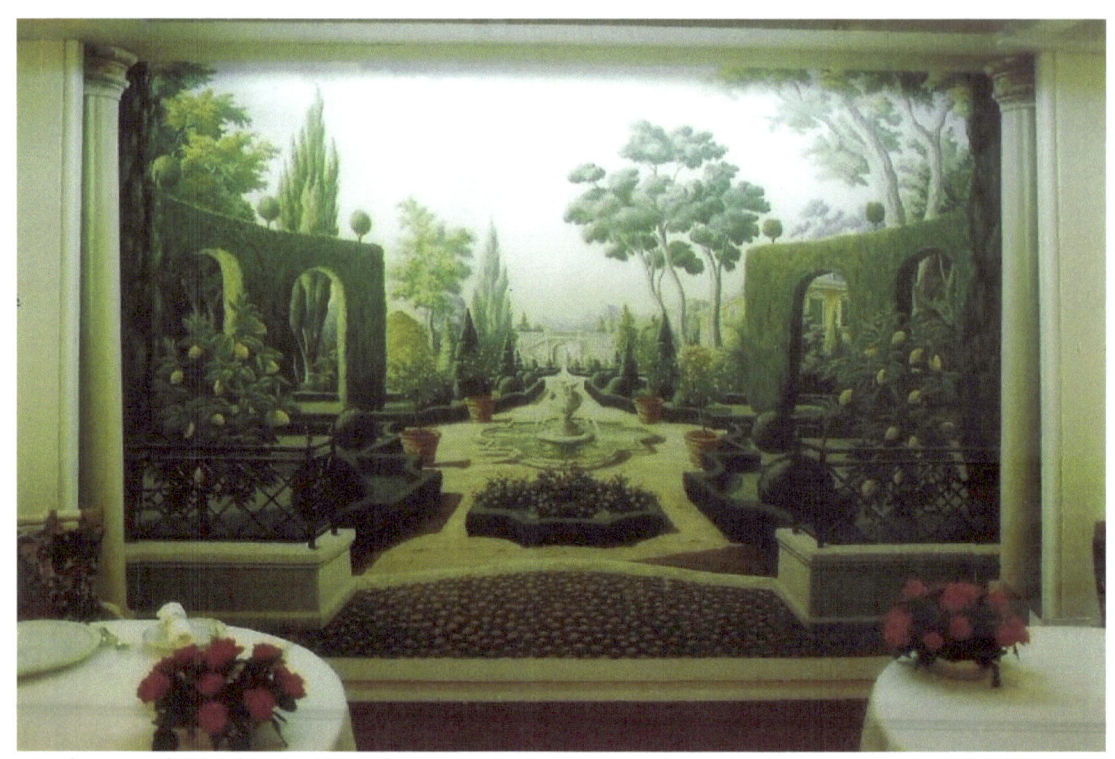

A formal Italian Garden, painted in a hotel dining room in Rome

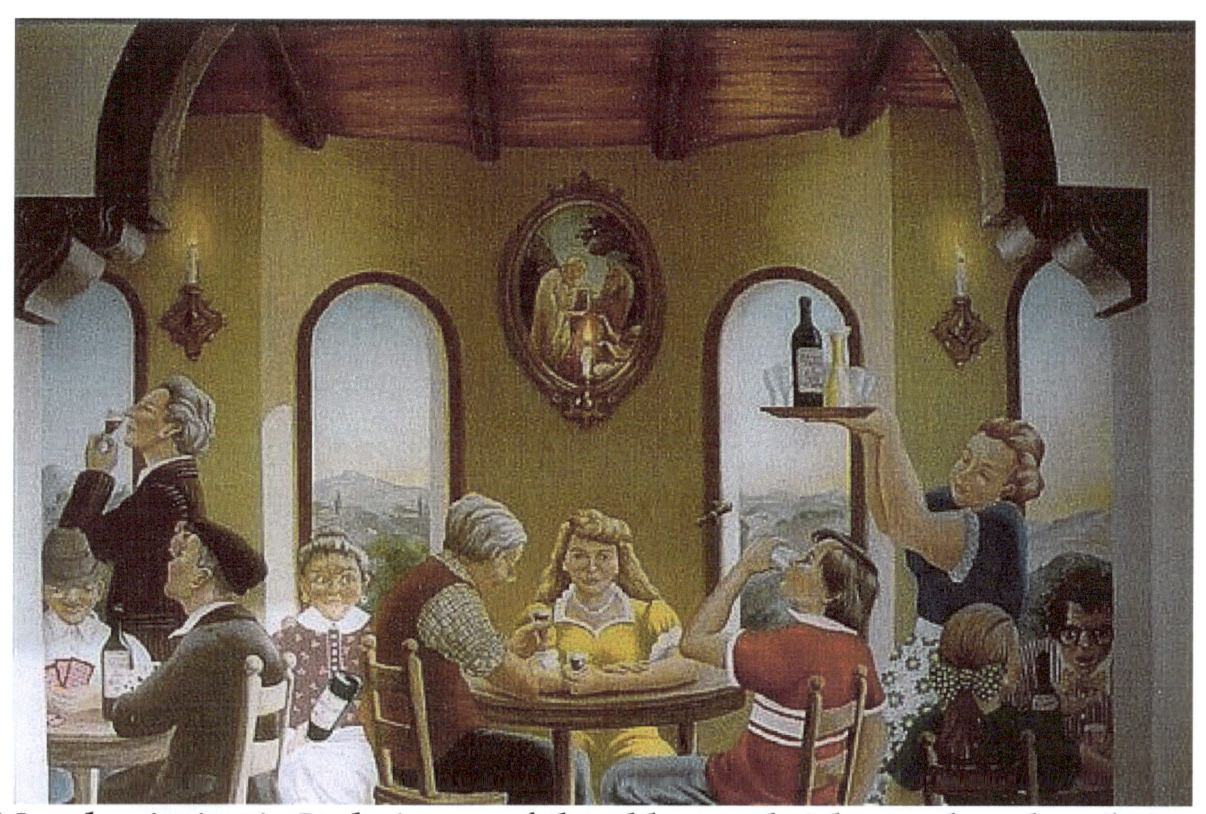

Mural painting in Italy is one of the oldest and richest cultural traditions of the western world, a bit like wine making really. This detail shows an icon of St. Martin, the patron saint of winemakers. He was a Roman soldier who cut his cloak in two and gave half to a beggar. It's bad luck if you drink the new wine before St. Martin's day!

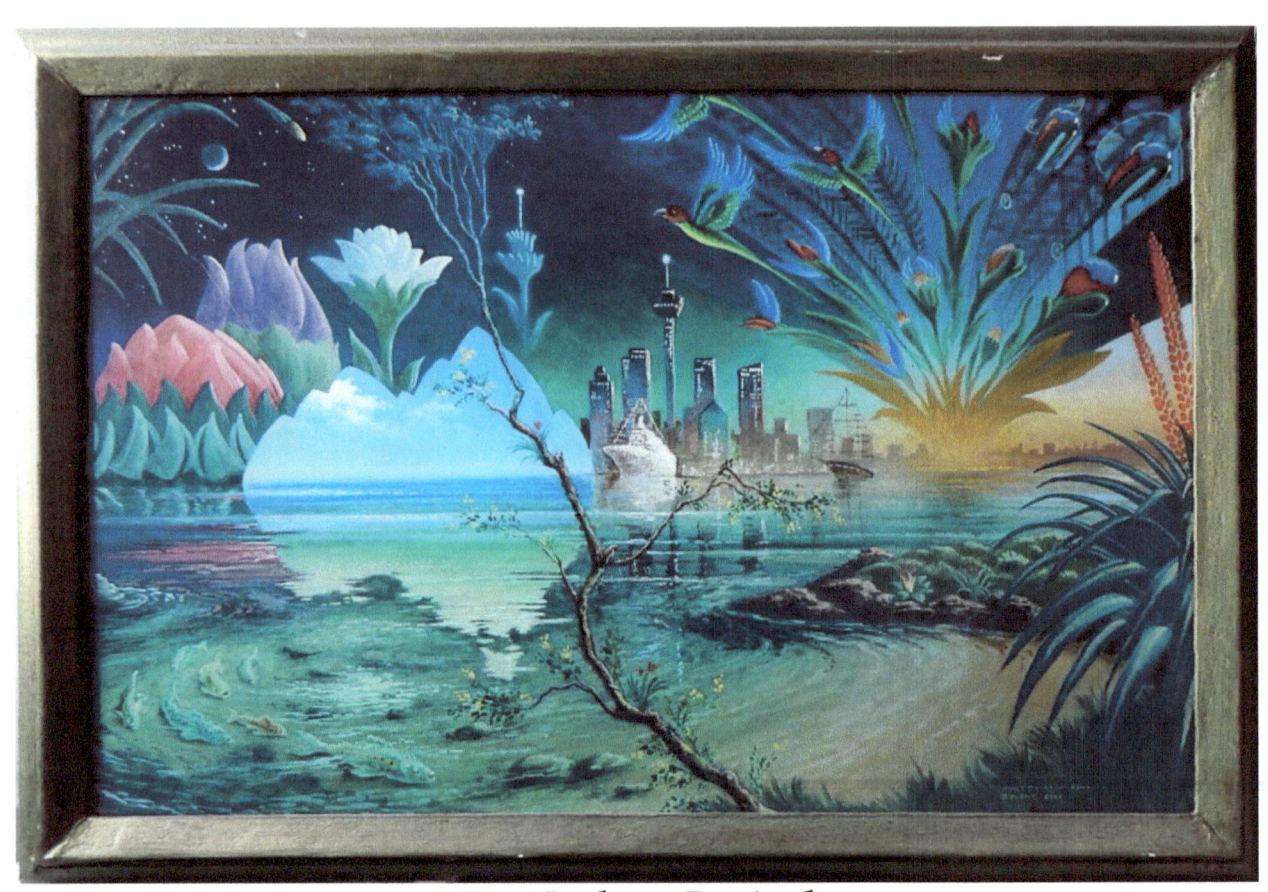

Port Jackson Revised

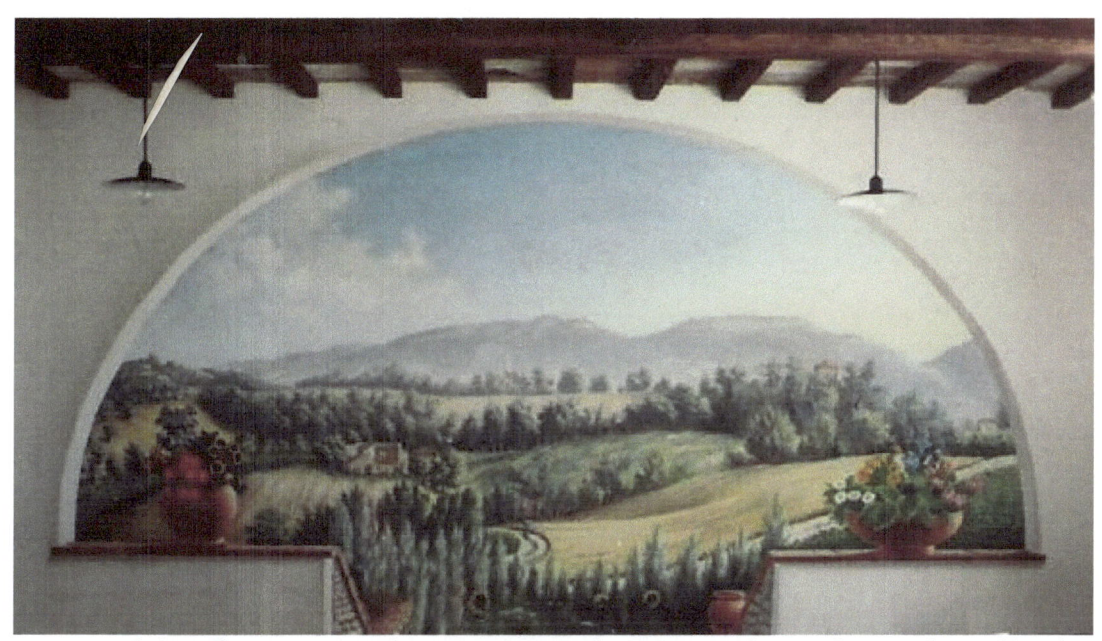

Local landscape with a wide arch, painted on the end wall of a Restaurant at San Bucetole in Umbria, Central Italy. 4x3m

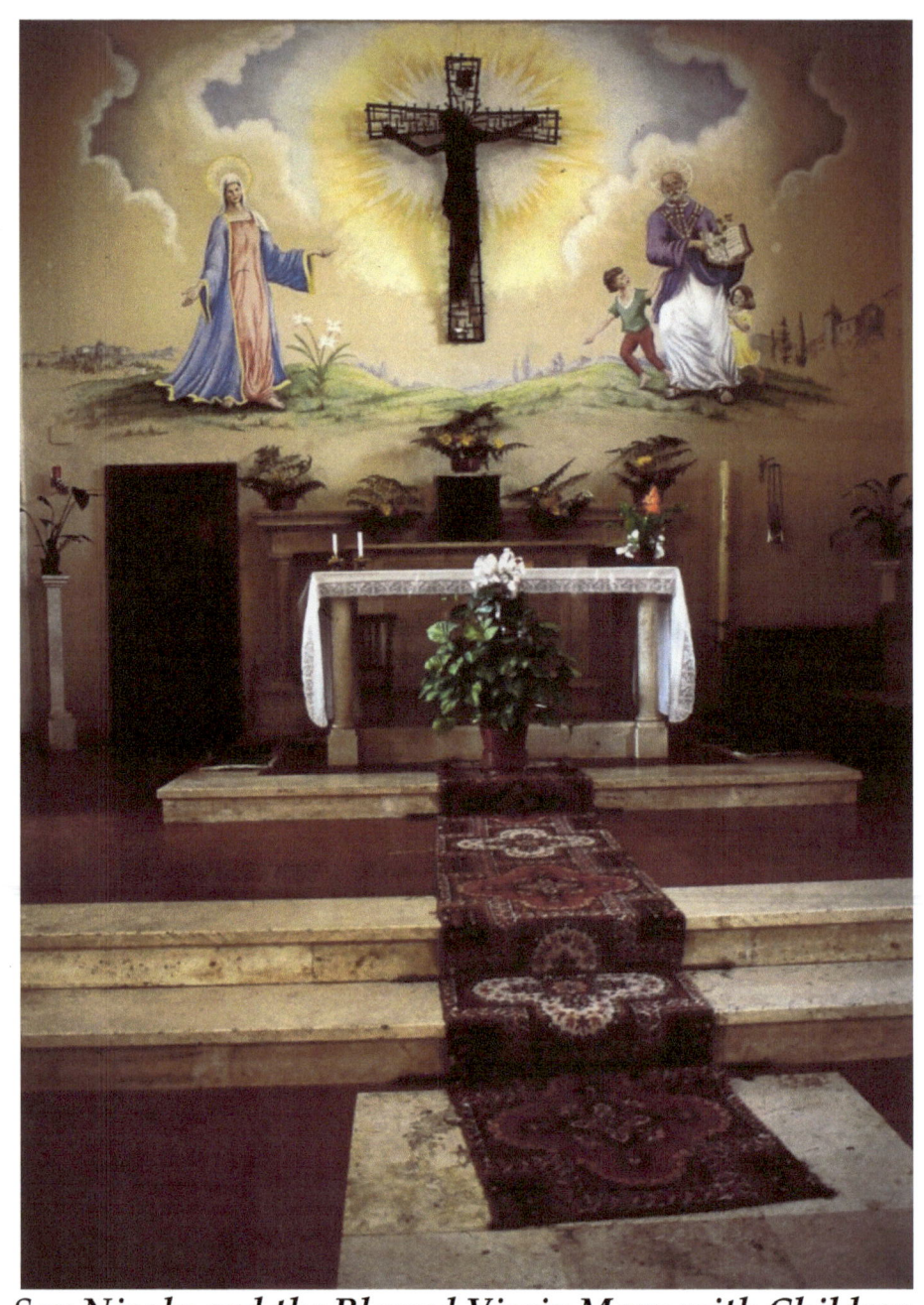

San Nicola and the Blessed Virgin Mary with Children.
Altarpiece painted at the Church of San Nicola in Macchie di Amelia,
Umbria, Central Italy. 5x4 m
(The iron cross was made from war debris by a local blacksmith)

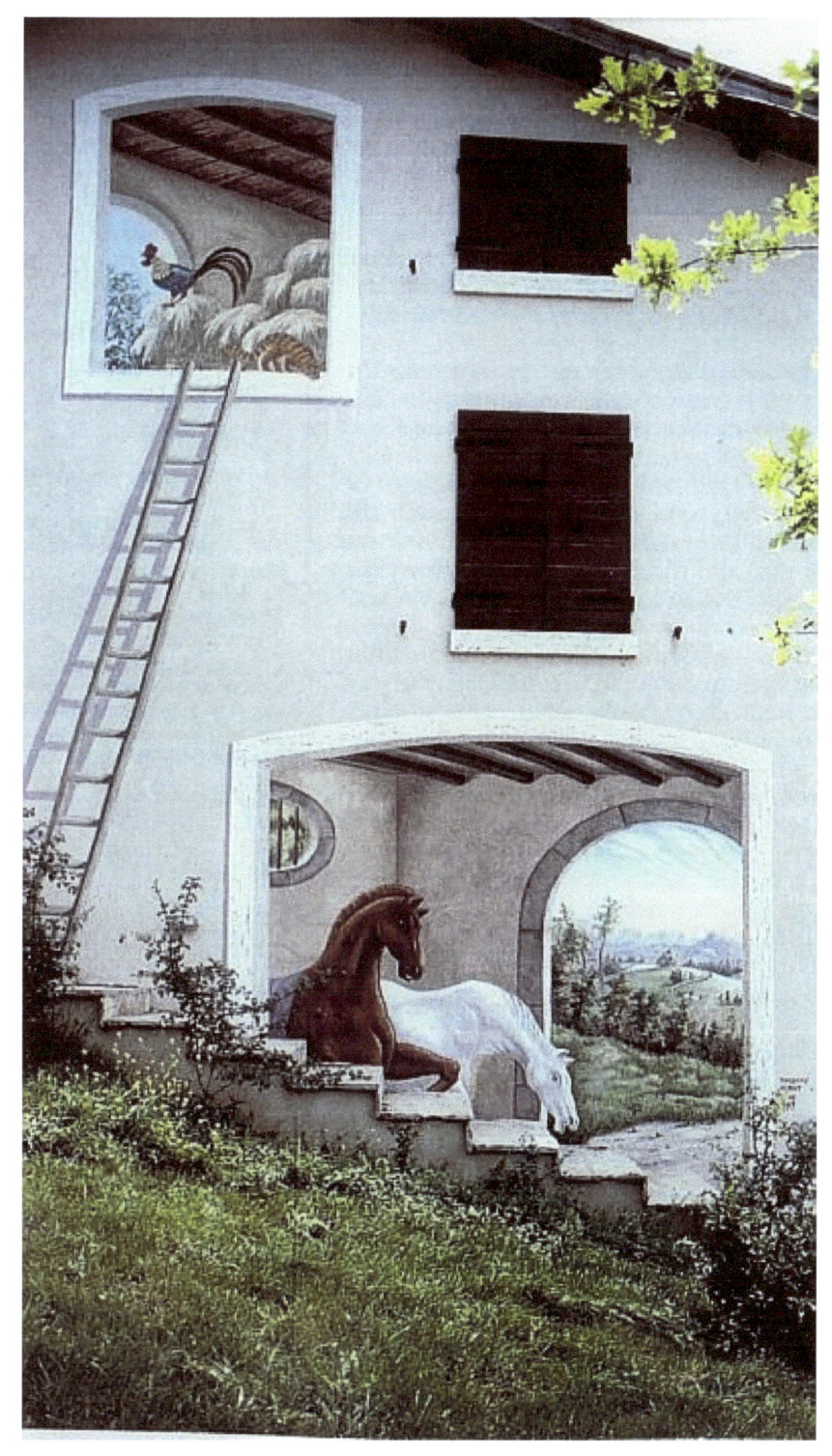

Farmyard Mural, Amelia, Italy, 8x4 m.

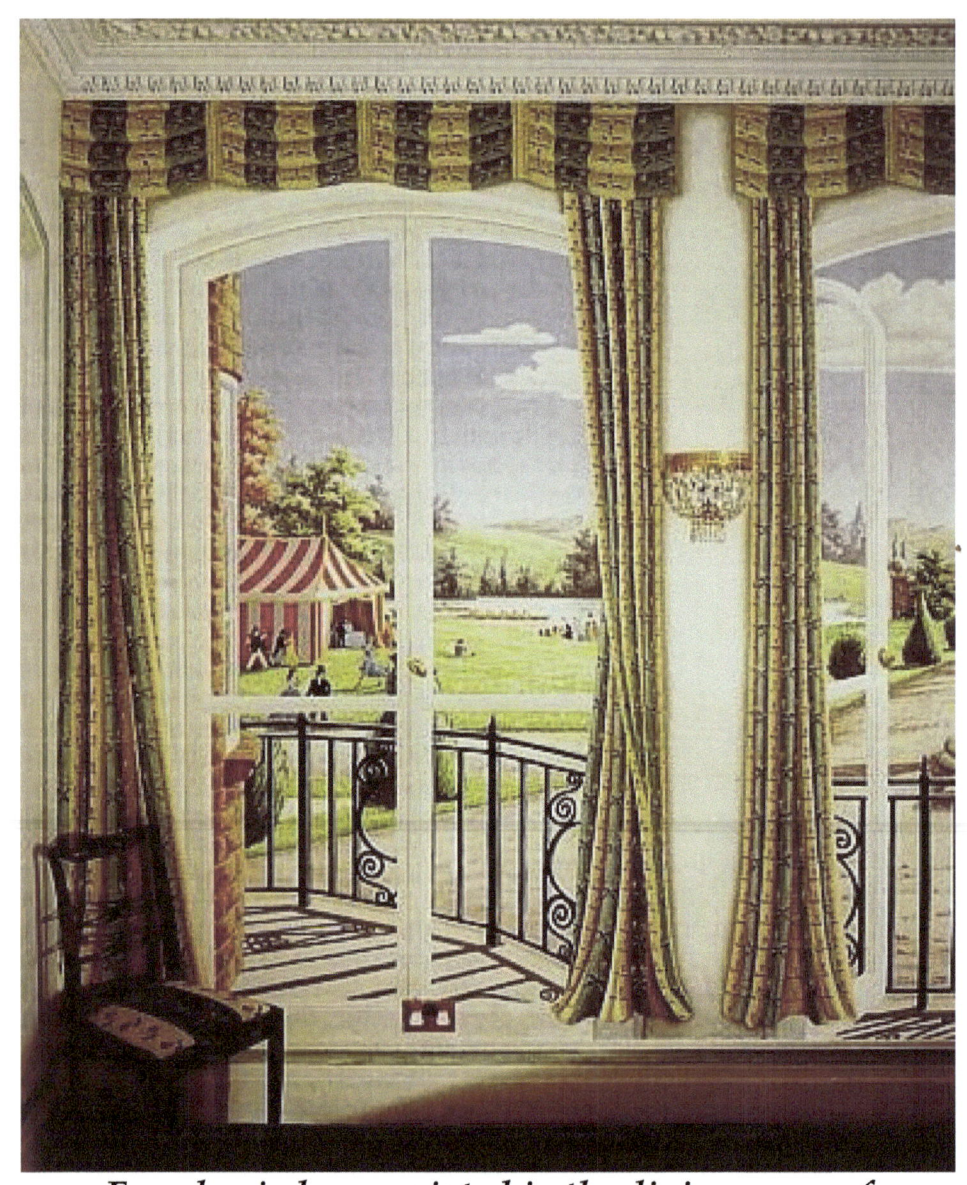

*French windows painted in the dining room of
a London town house. 8x3,5m*

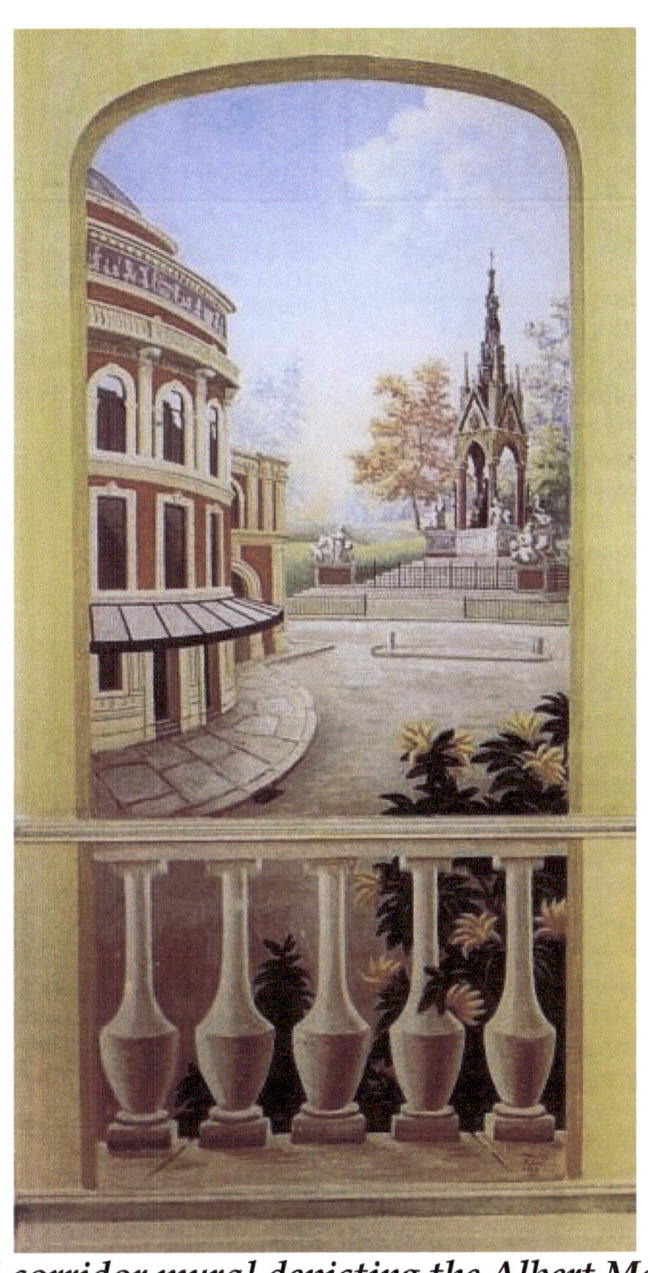

End-of-corridor mural depicting the Albert Memorial and the Royal Albert Hall, painted in a flat next to the Royal Albert Hall, London, England 3x1.5m

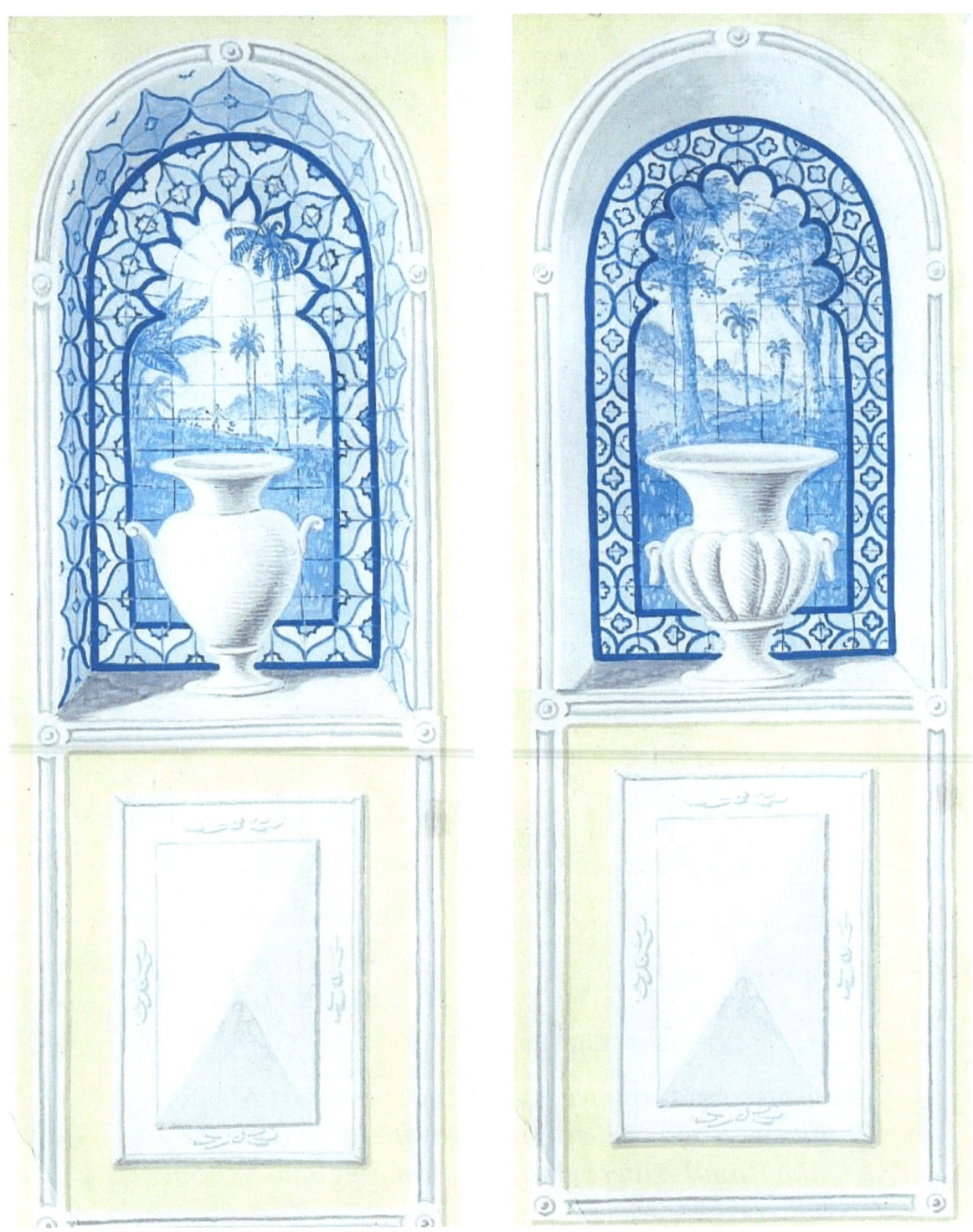

A pair of alcoves in the azulejo style

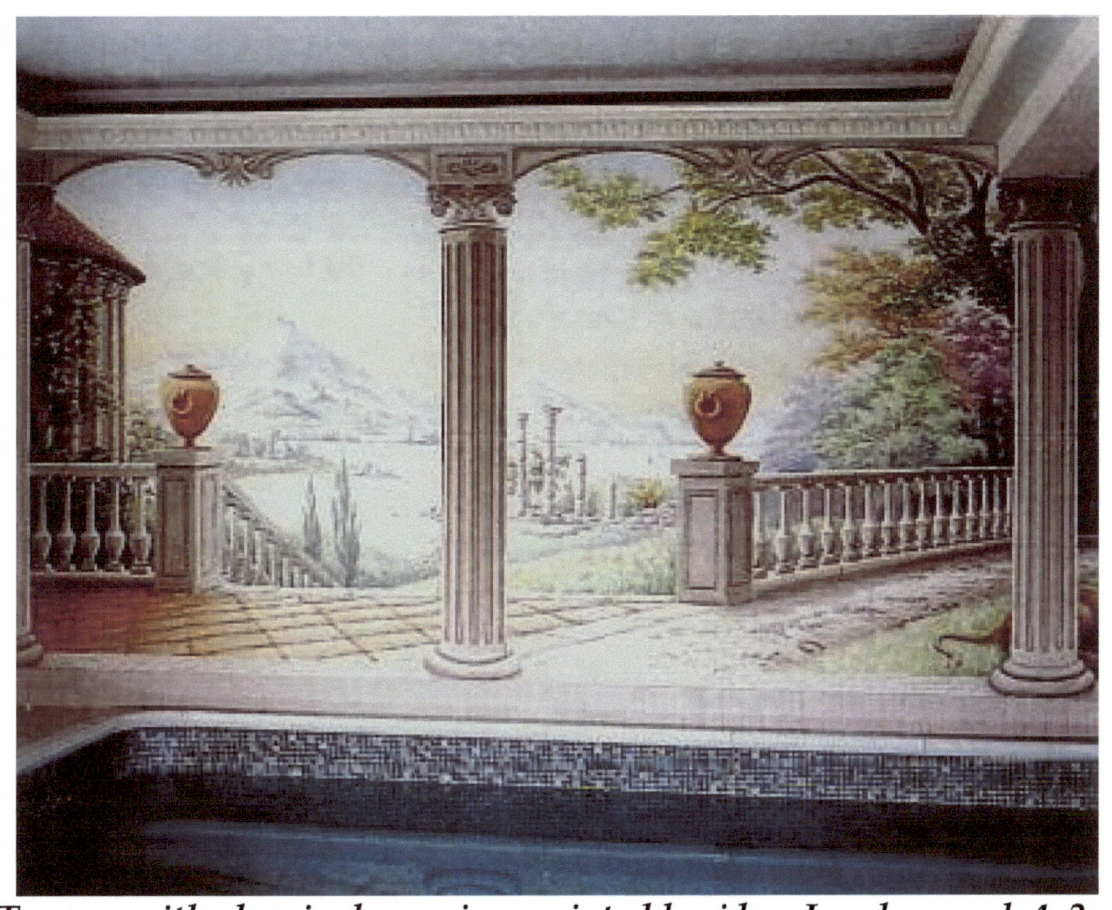

Terrace with classical remains, painted beside a London pool. 4x3m

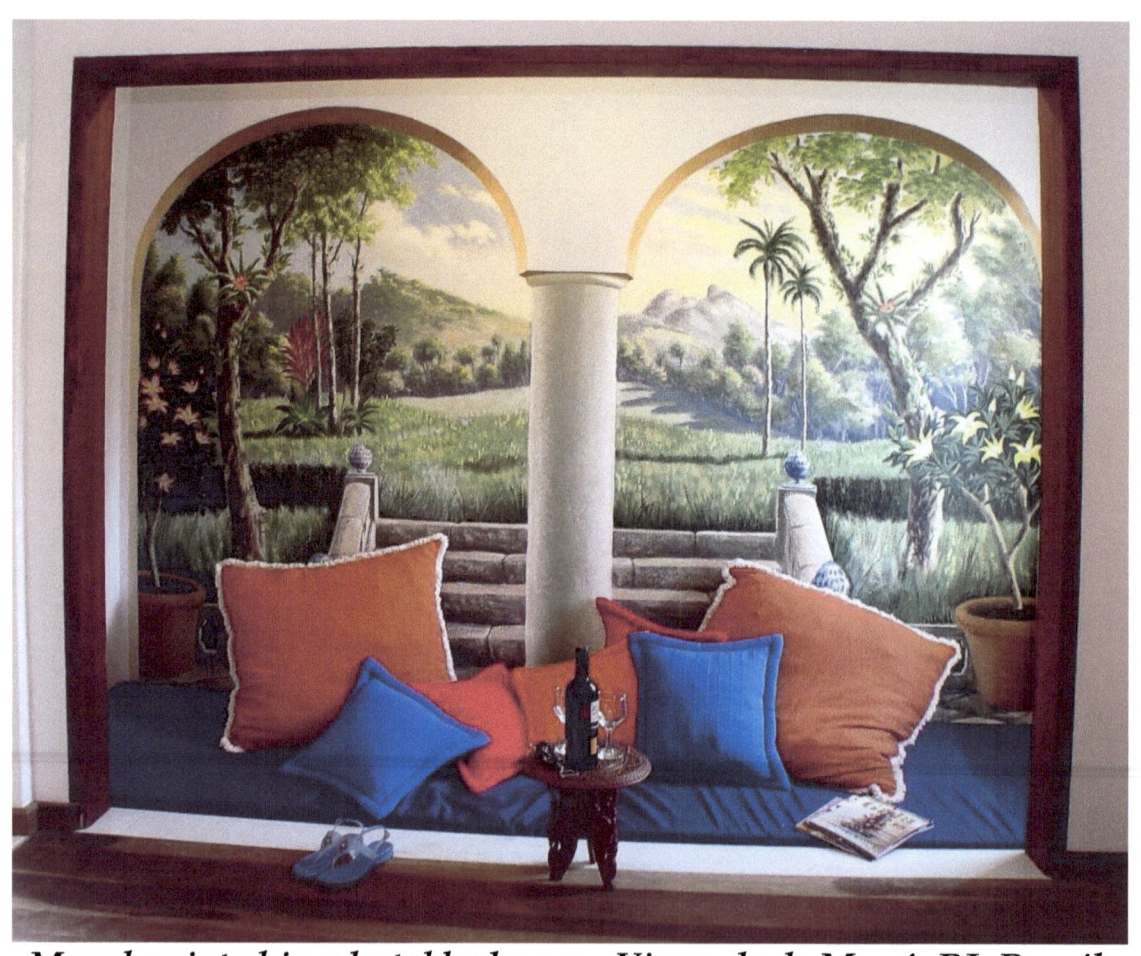

Mural painted in a hotel bedroom , Visconde de Mauá, RJ, Brazil.

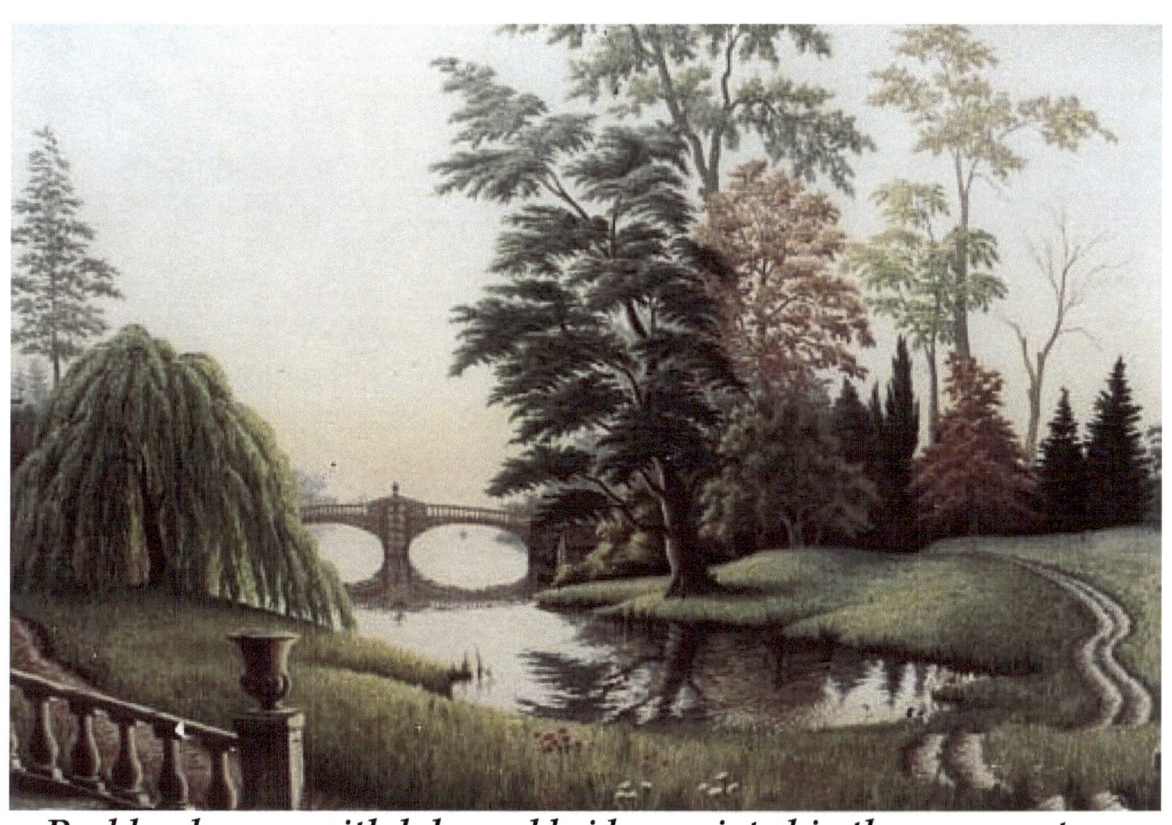

Parkland scene with lake and bridge, painted in the conservatory of a town house, London, England

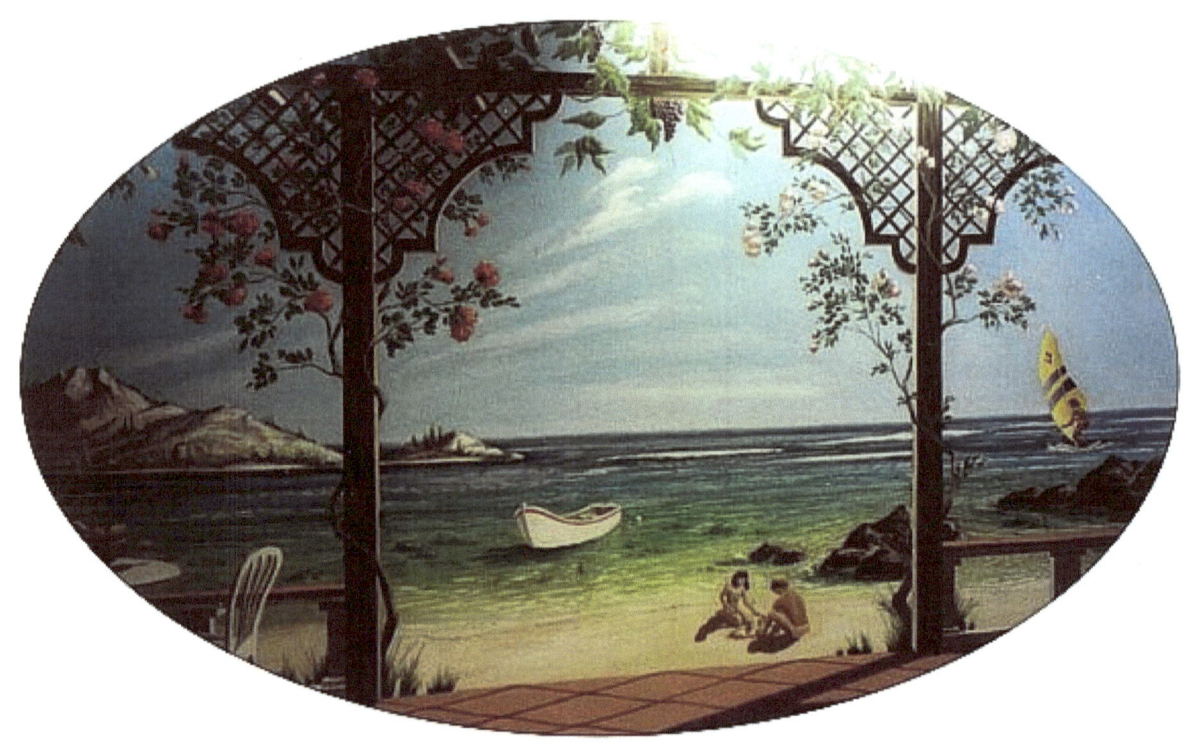

Hellenic beach scene, painted in a corridor at Queen's Hospital, Burton-upon-Trent. 3x2.5m

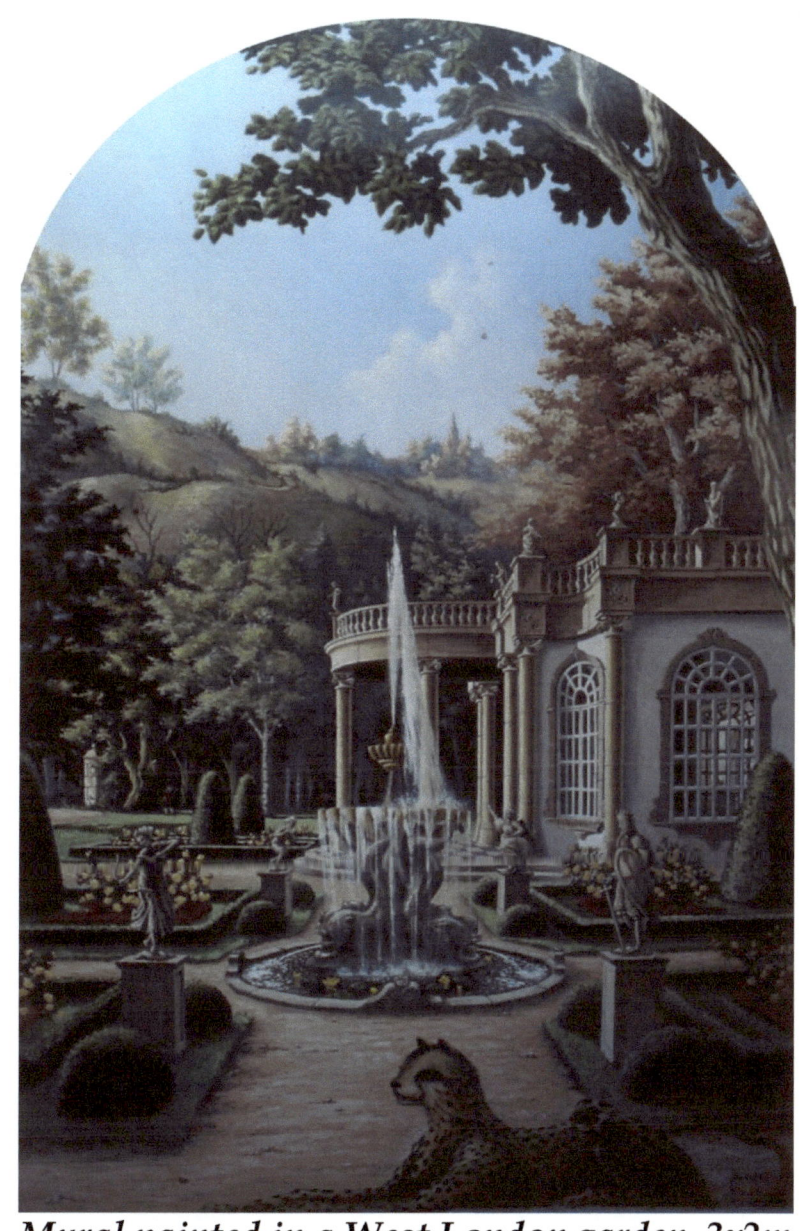

Mural painted in a West London garden. 3x2m

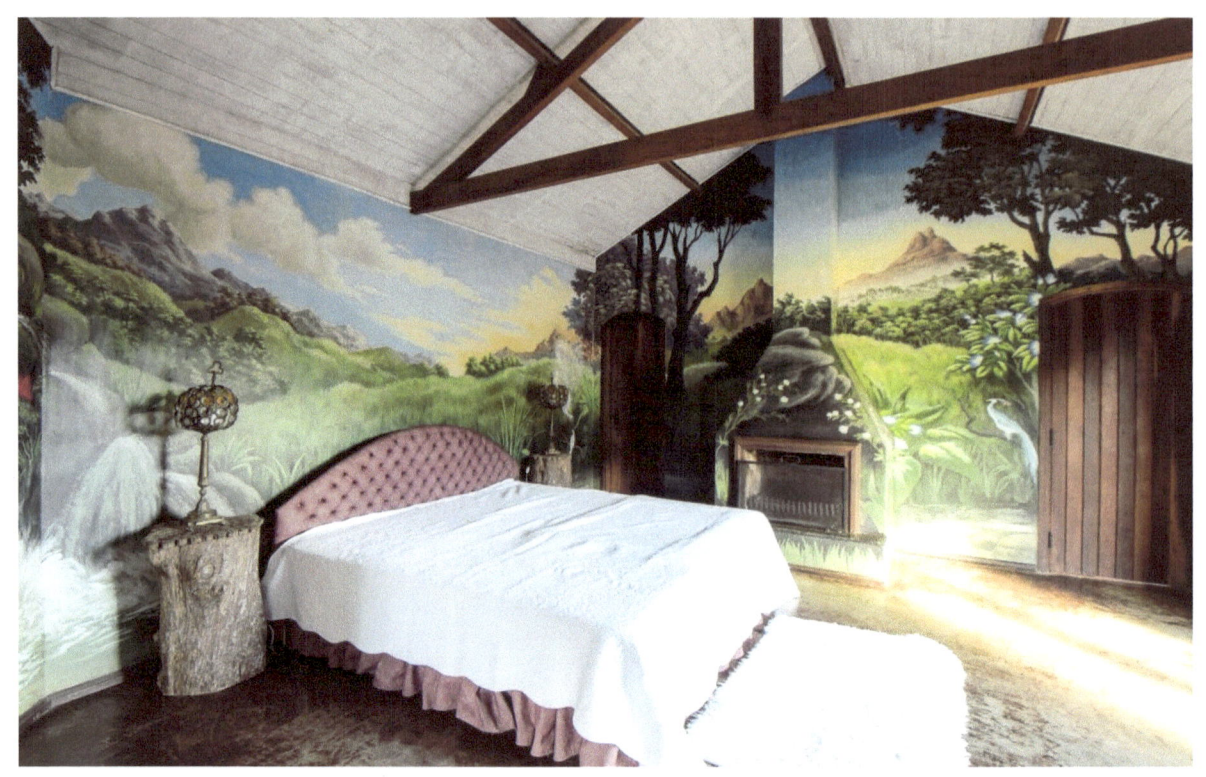

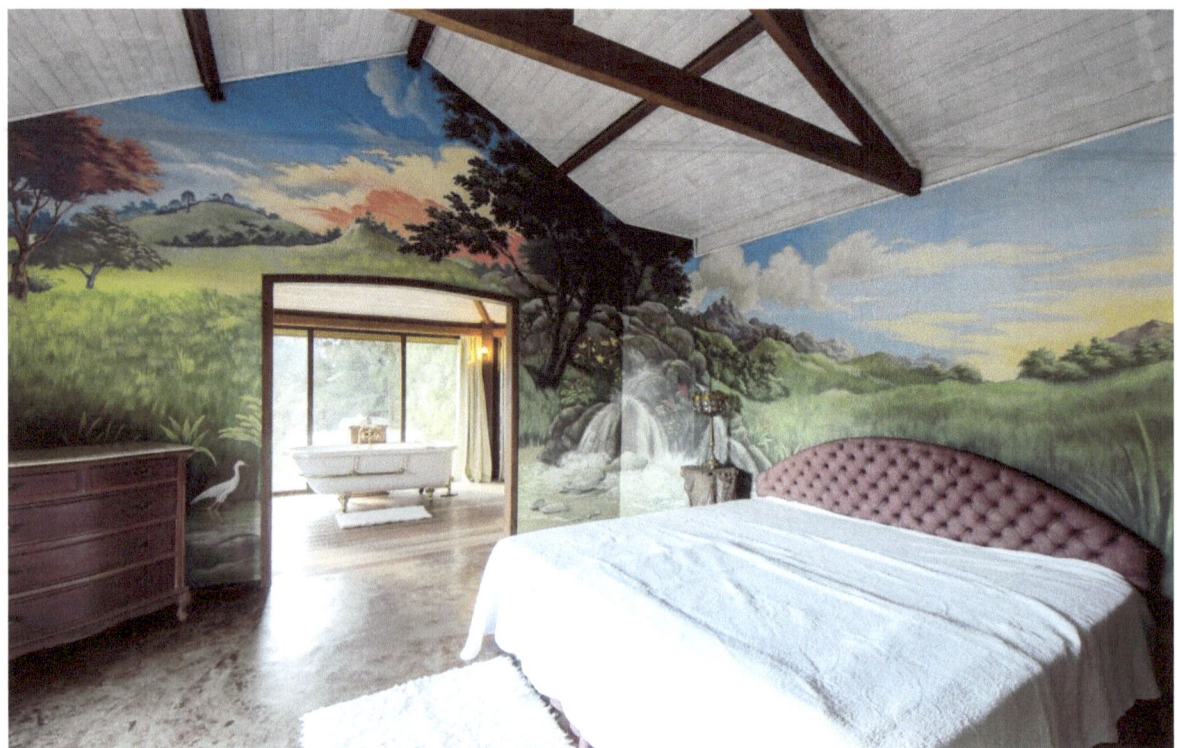

The Fronteira Murals – The Garden of God 1 & 2

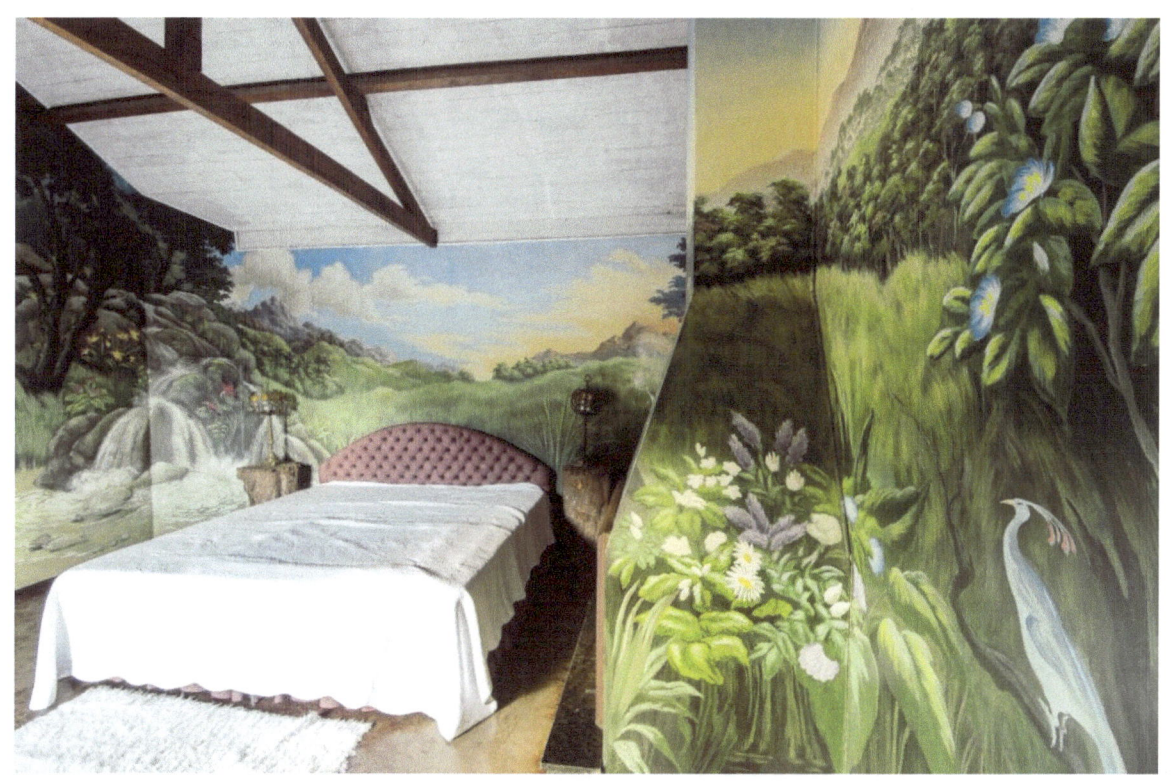

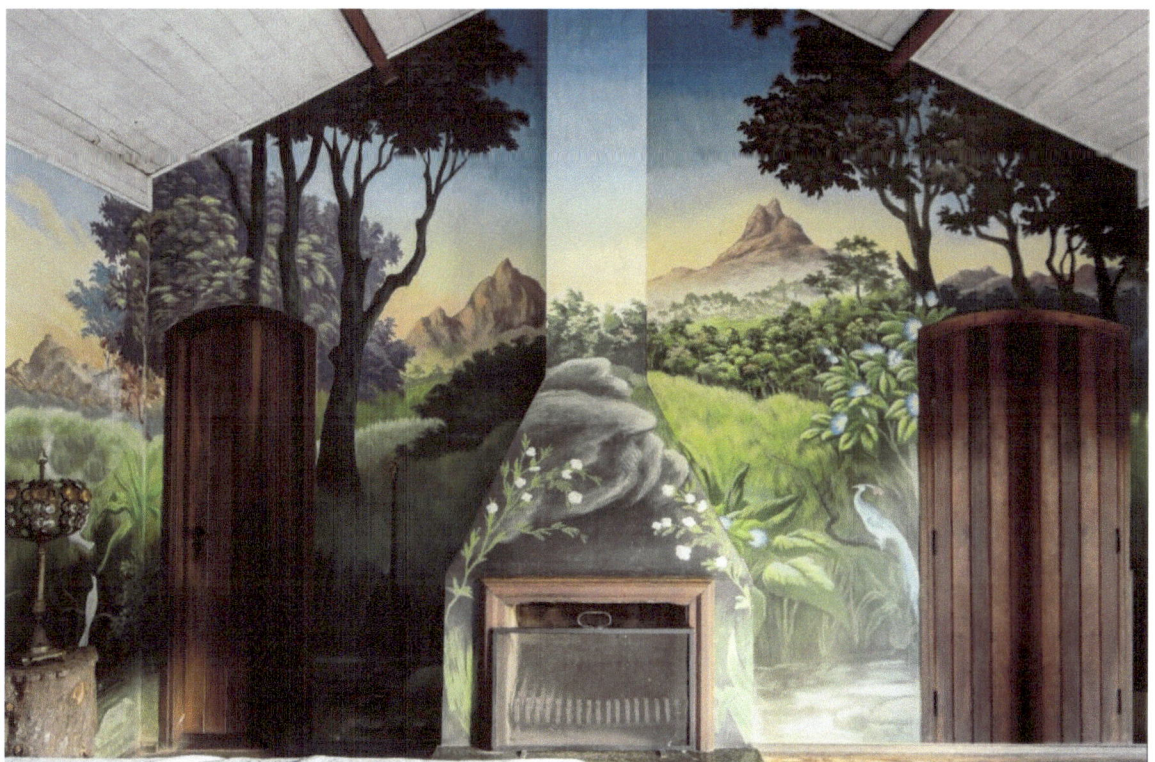

The Fronteira Murals – The Garden of God 3 & 4

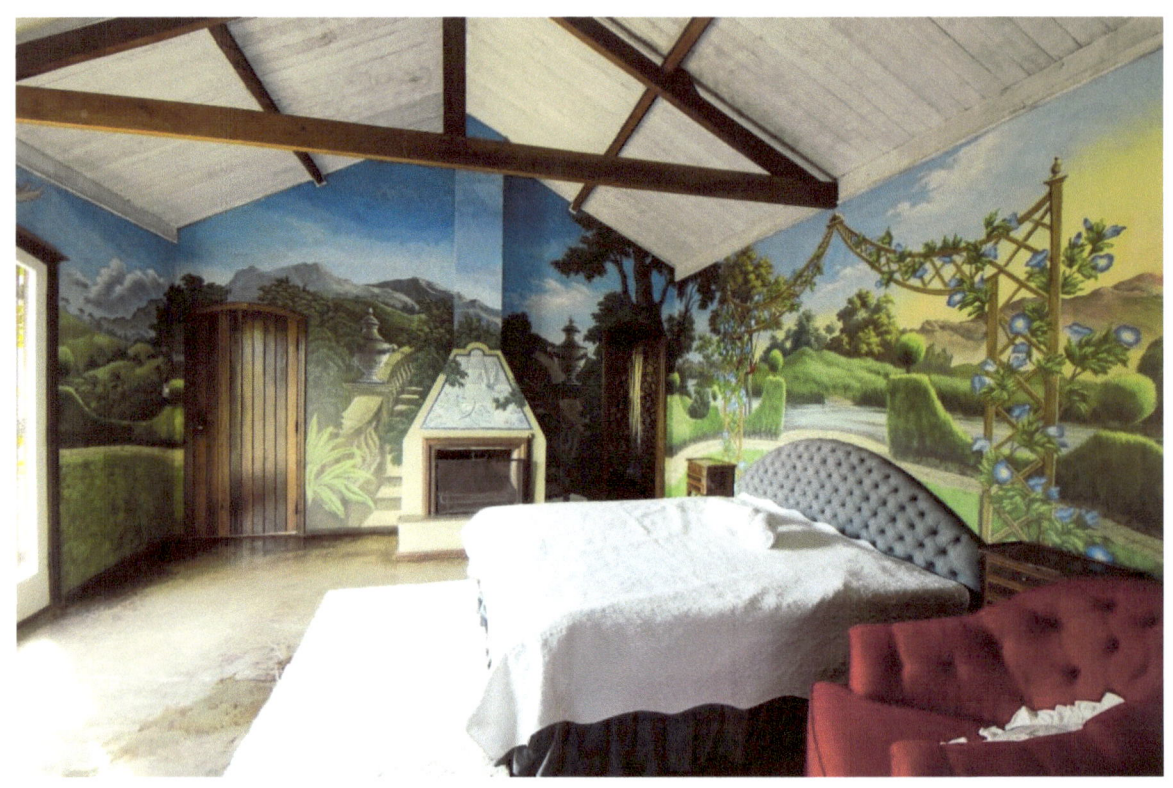

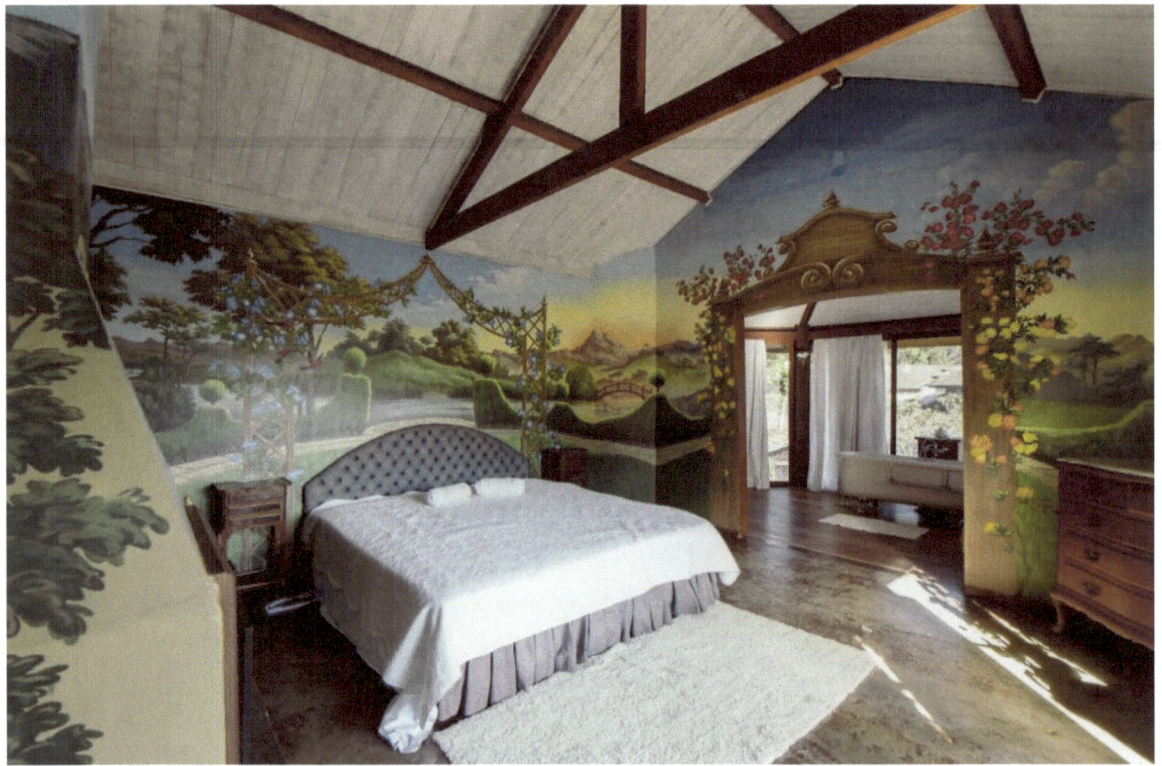

The Fronteira Murals – The Garden of Man 1 & 2

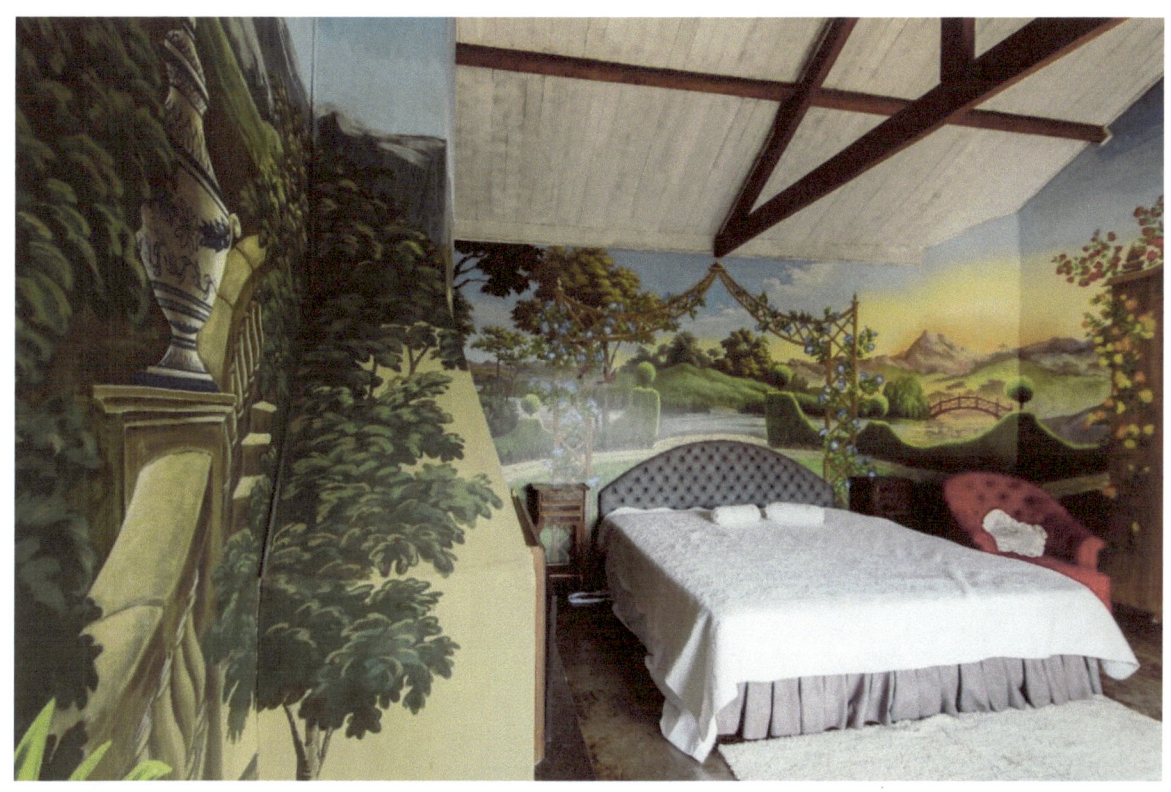

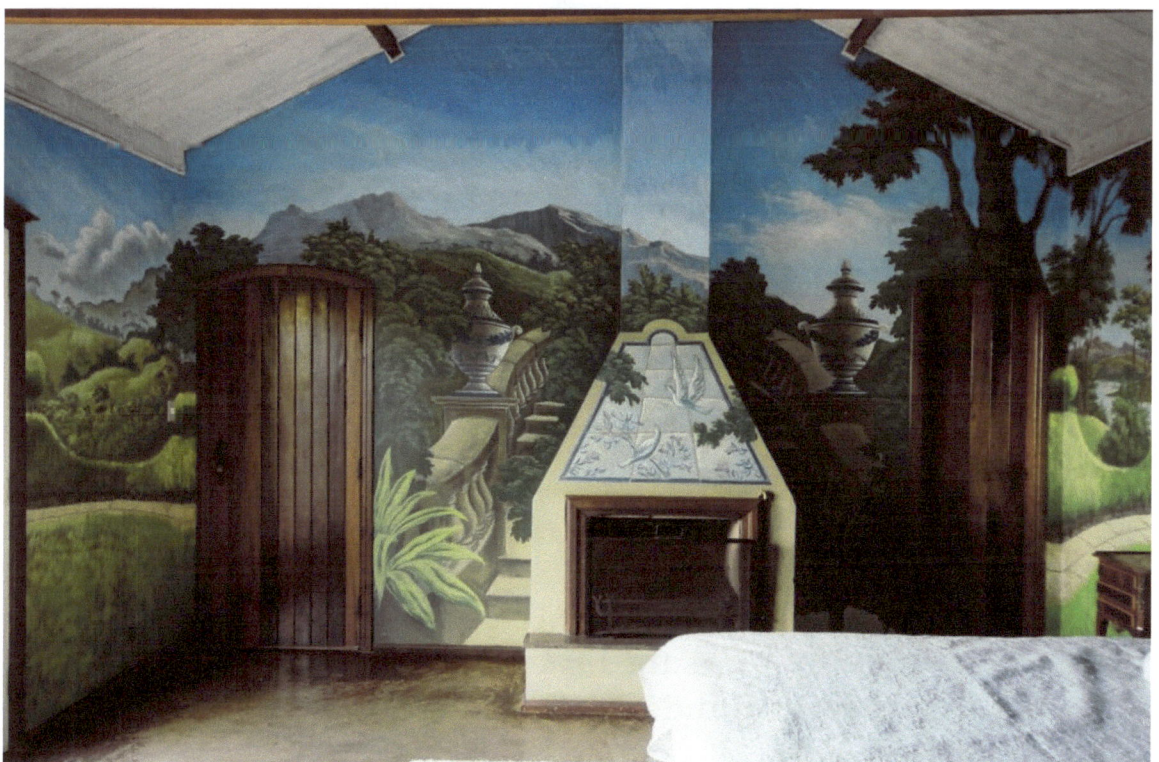

The Fronteira Murals – The Garden of Man 3 & 4

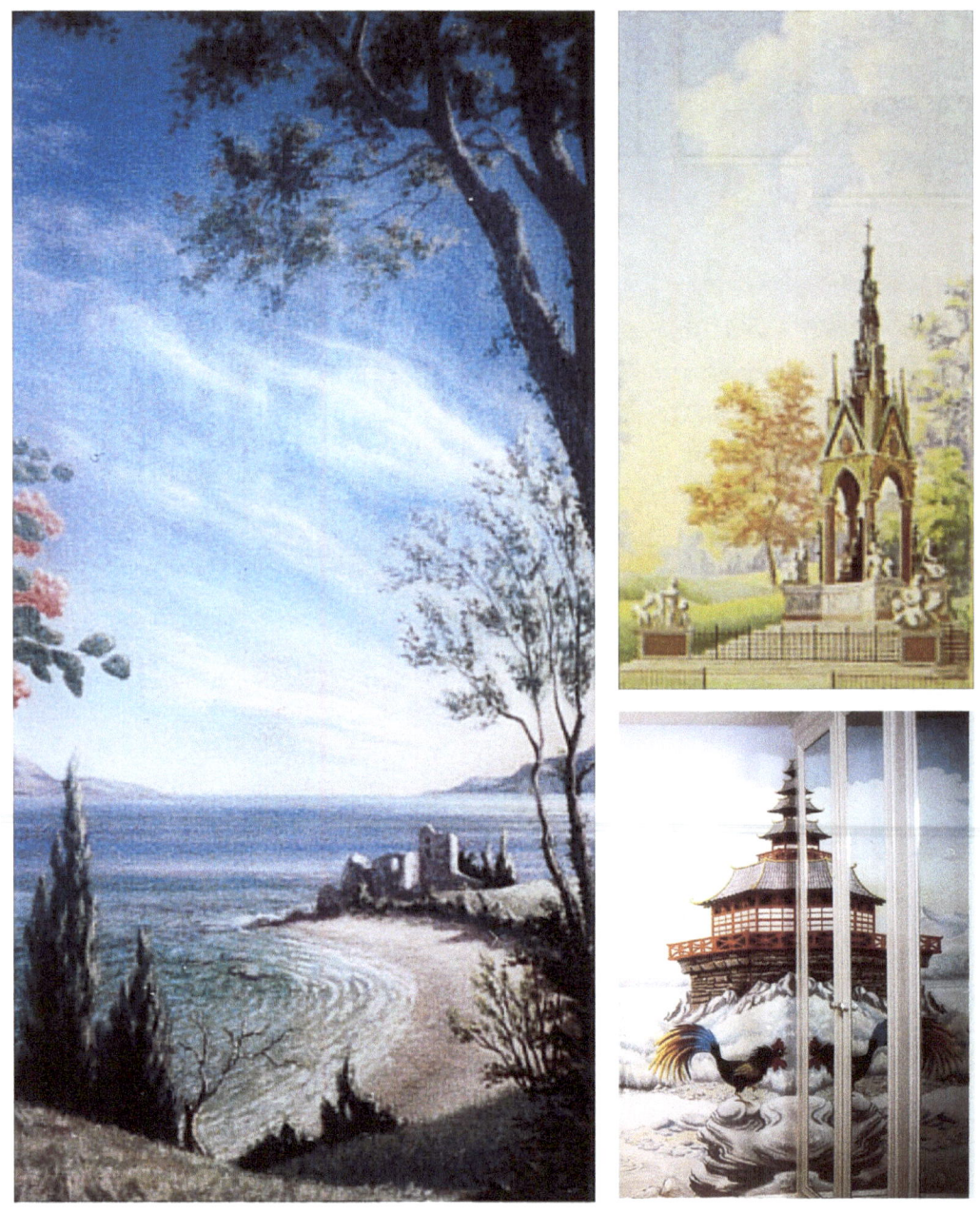

Structures in a lanscape: Headland Castle. The Albert Memorial, one of the greatest follies of them all, and half a pagoda with one fighting cock – the wardrobe mirror does the rest. Note the rock formation in the foreground of the pagoda mural.

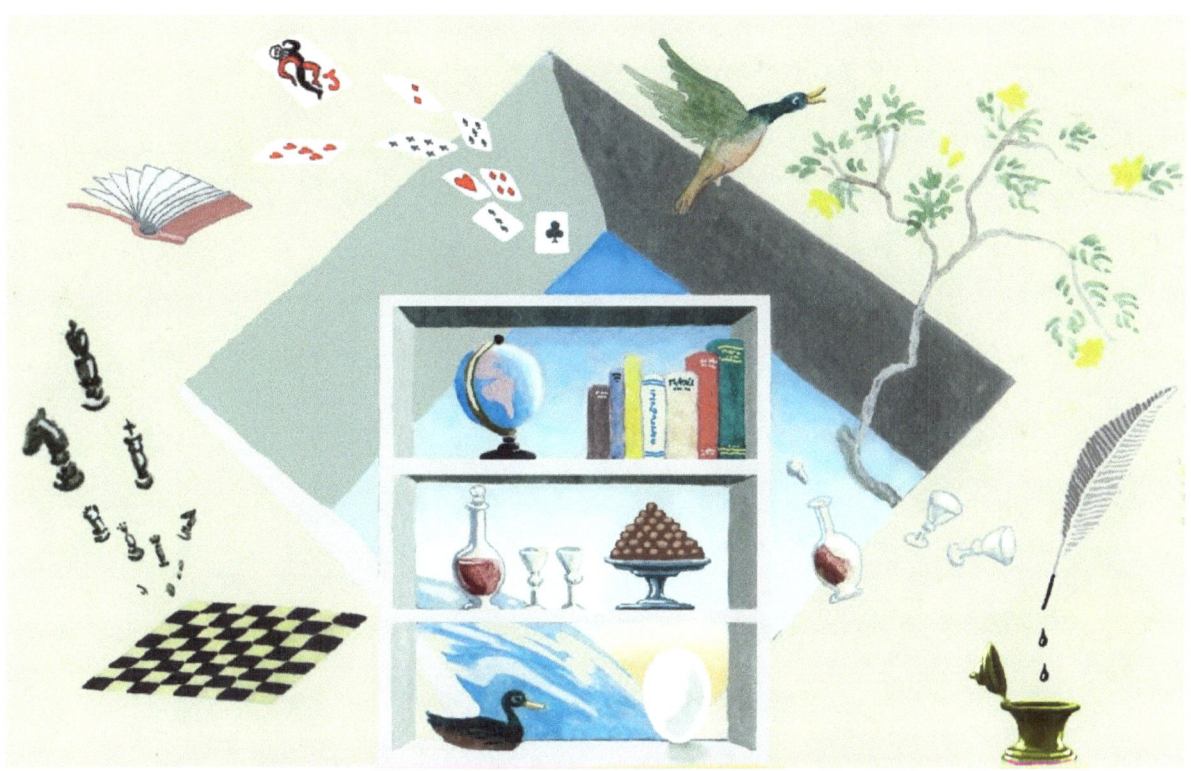

Design for a mural – A library of the mind

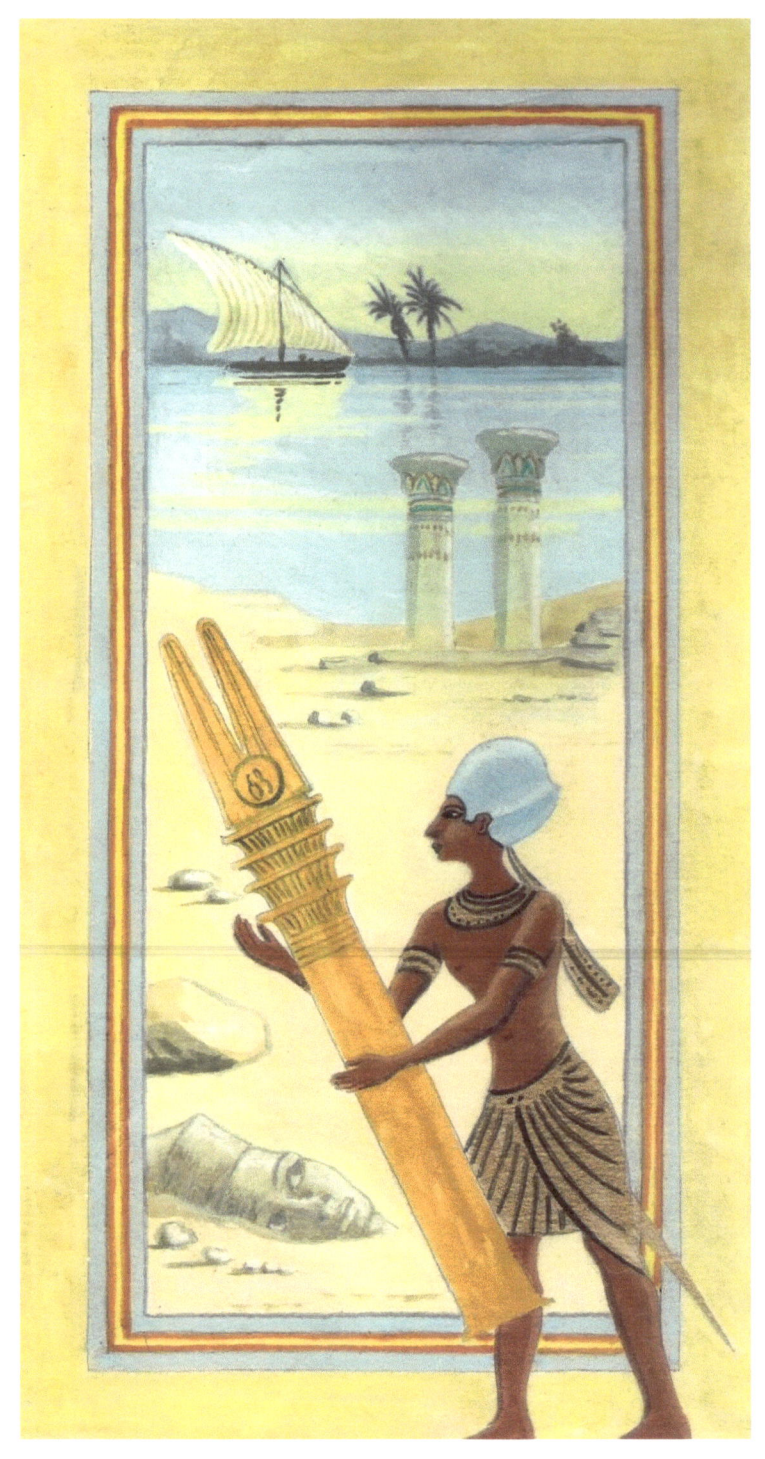

Design for a Mural – Nile Walker

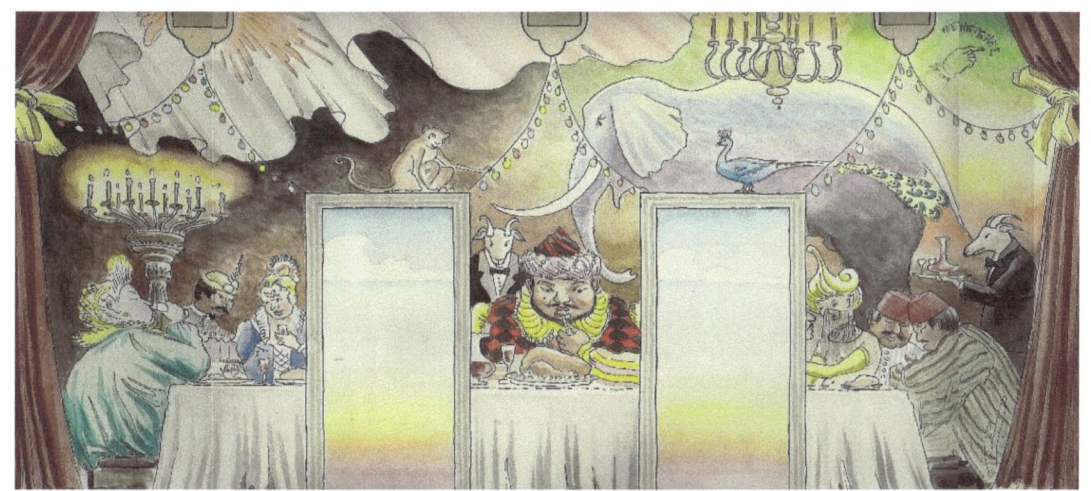

Design for a mural – Nebuchadnezzar's Feast

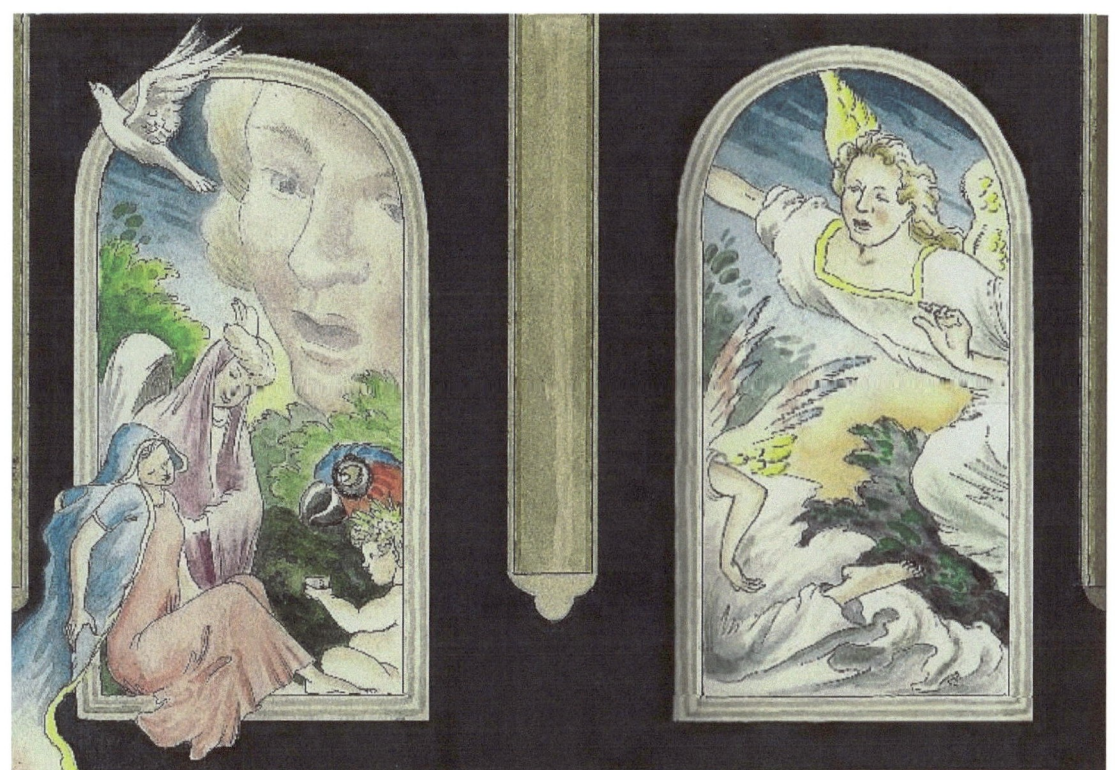

Desigh for a mural – The Annunciation (both of the above themes were done for the Limelight mural in São Paulo, Brazil)

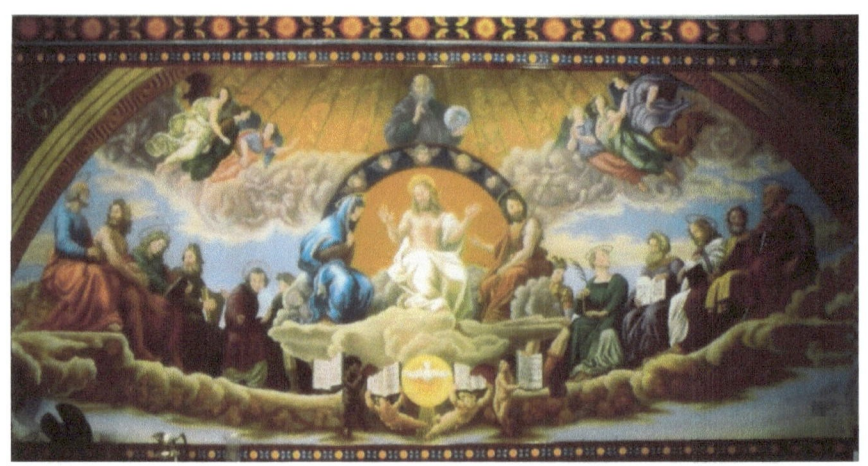

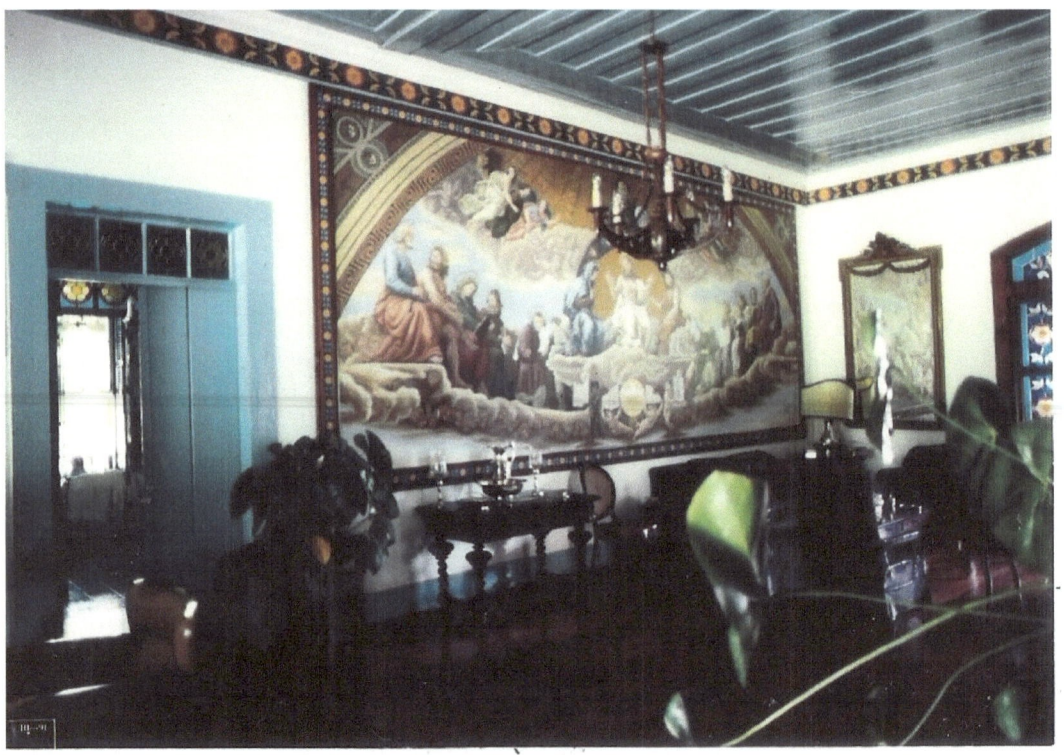

Homage to Raphael – an interpretation of one of his Vatican murals painted at a Brazilian plantation house. 6x3m

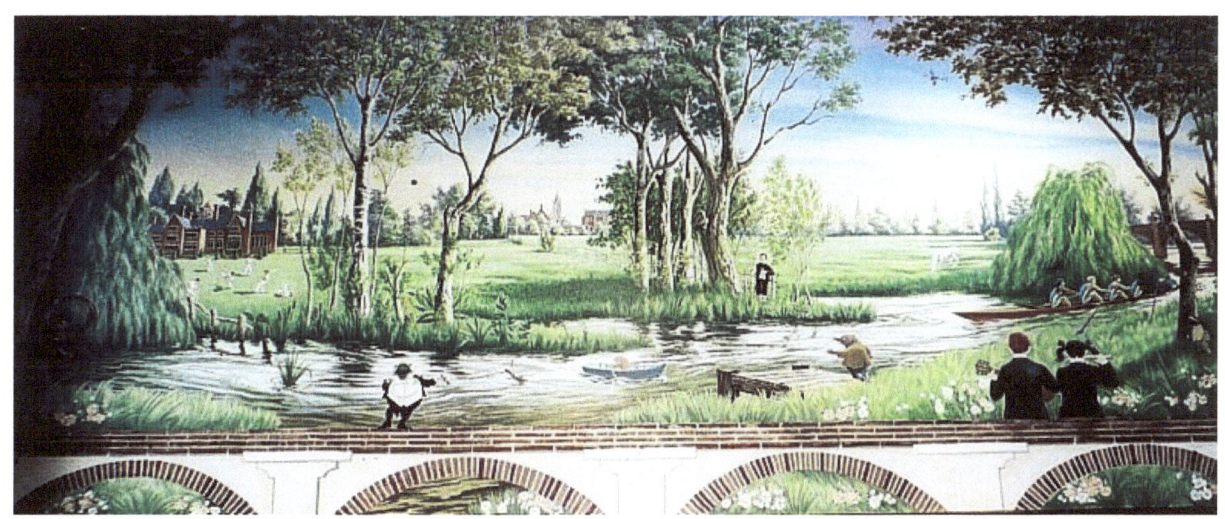

Panoramic landscape with sporting and literary figures, painted in the dining hall at St Edward's School, Oxford. 8x3m

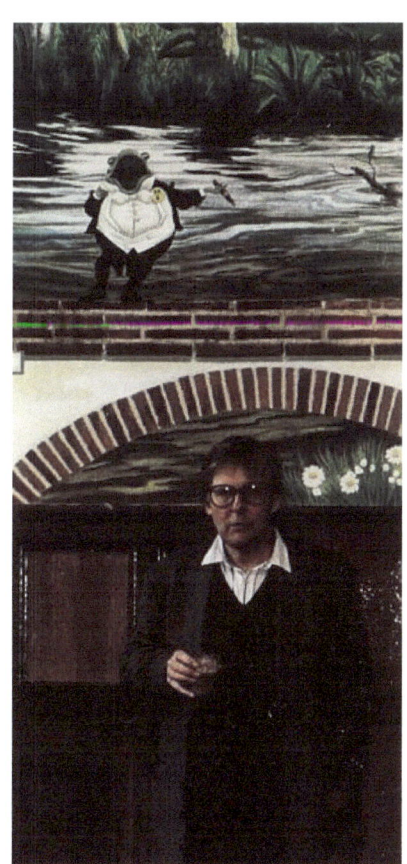

This work was painted as a tribute to Kenneth Graham and E.H. Shepherd

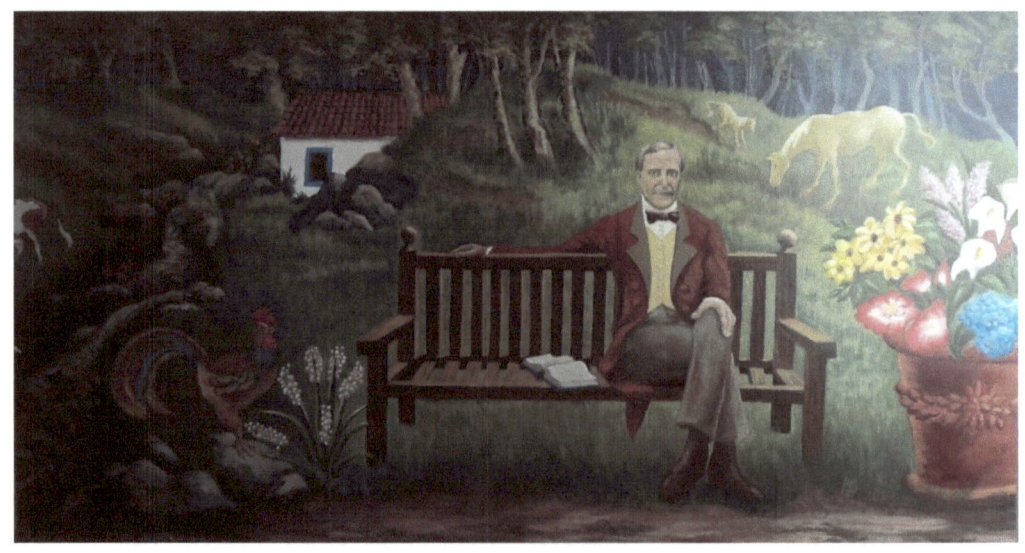

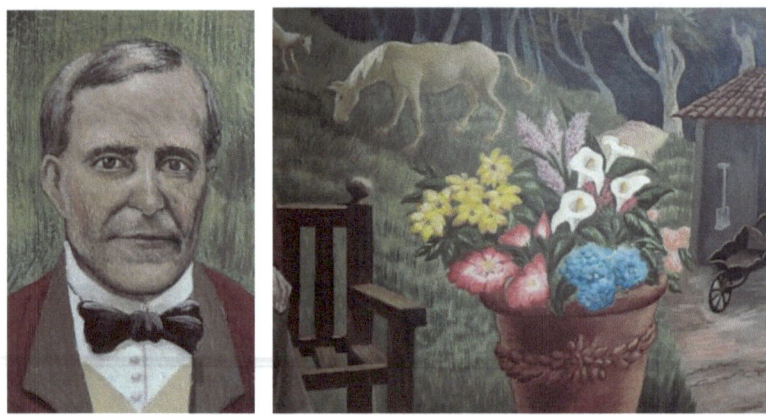

Portrait of the Visconde de Mauá, painted at the Aldeia dos Imigrantes shopping centre, Visconde de Mauá, RJ, Brasil.

Irineu Evangelista de Souza, Visconde de Mauá, (1813 – 1889) received the lands around Visconde de Mauá as a concession from the Imperial Government of Brazil, but apparently never visited the place himself. His son Henrique installed the first colony, of mainly German and Swiss farmers, and named it after his father. The name of Visconde de Mauá is naturally quite familiar to the inhabitants and the many tourists who come here, but the personal appearance of the Visconde is not … or at least it wasn't until now. The Visconde de Mauá was the most successful and celebrated businessman, banker and civil-engineering entrepreneur during the latter part of the Empire, but his powerful position did not endear him to the Emperor, Dom Pedro II. Even his title was less than complimentary, since Mauá is not one of the prettiest neighbourhoods in Rio. At one point the Visconde sent a beautiful wheel barrow made of Jacaranda and a silver spade as a present to the Emperor, to remind him of 'the value of sweated labour' (see detail below). After the declaration of the Republic, Dom Pedro II went into exile and died at the Hotel Bristol in Paris, lying on a pillow filled with Brazilian soil. Could it be that he used the silver spade to fill the pillow himself? One wonders.

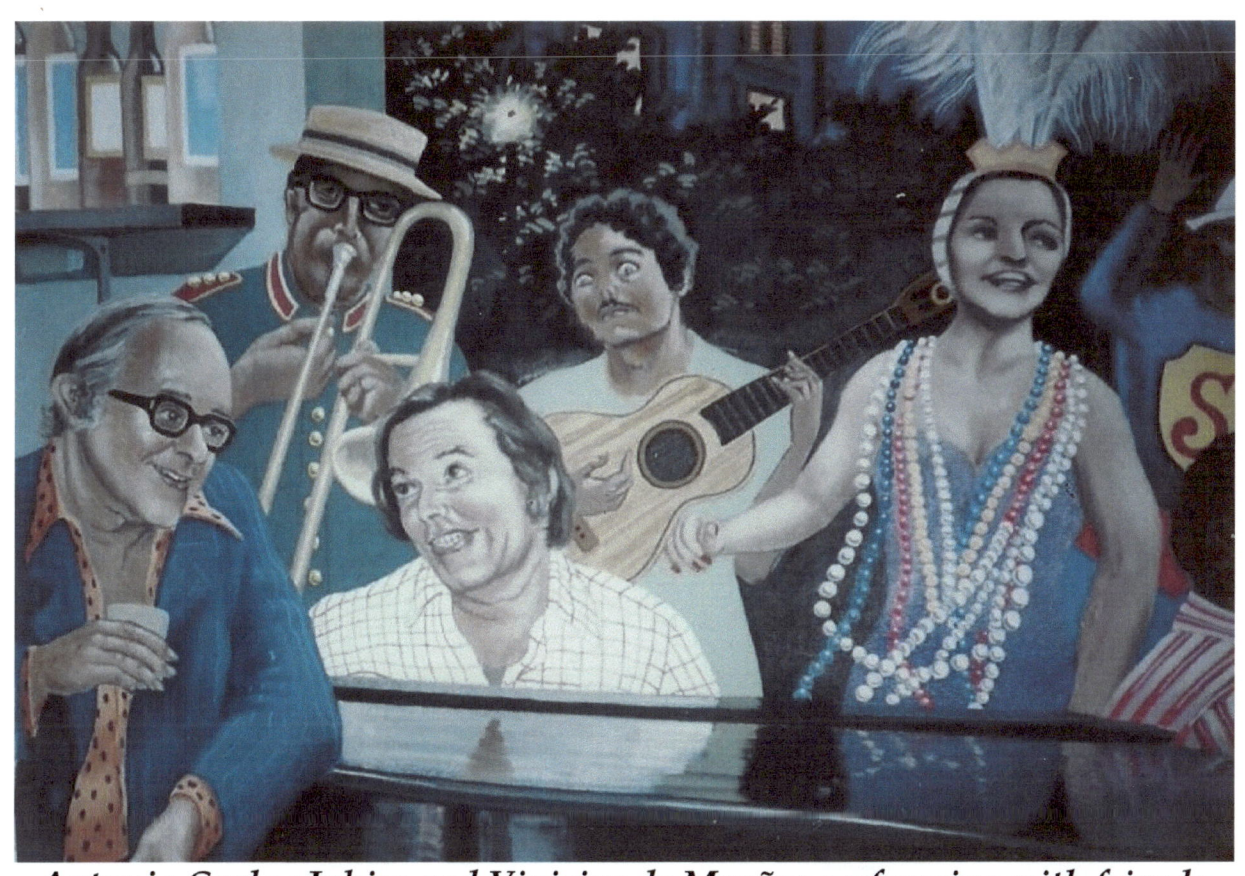

Antonio Carlos Jobim and Vinicius de Morães performing with friends at the Bofetada in Rio. 3x2m

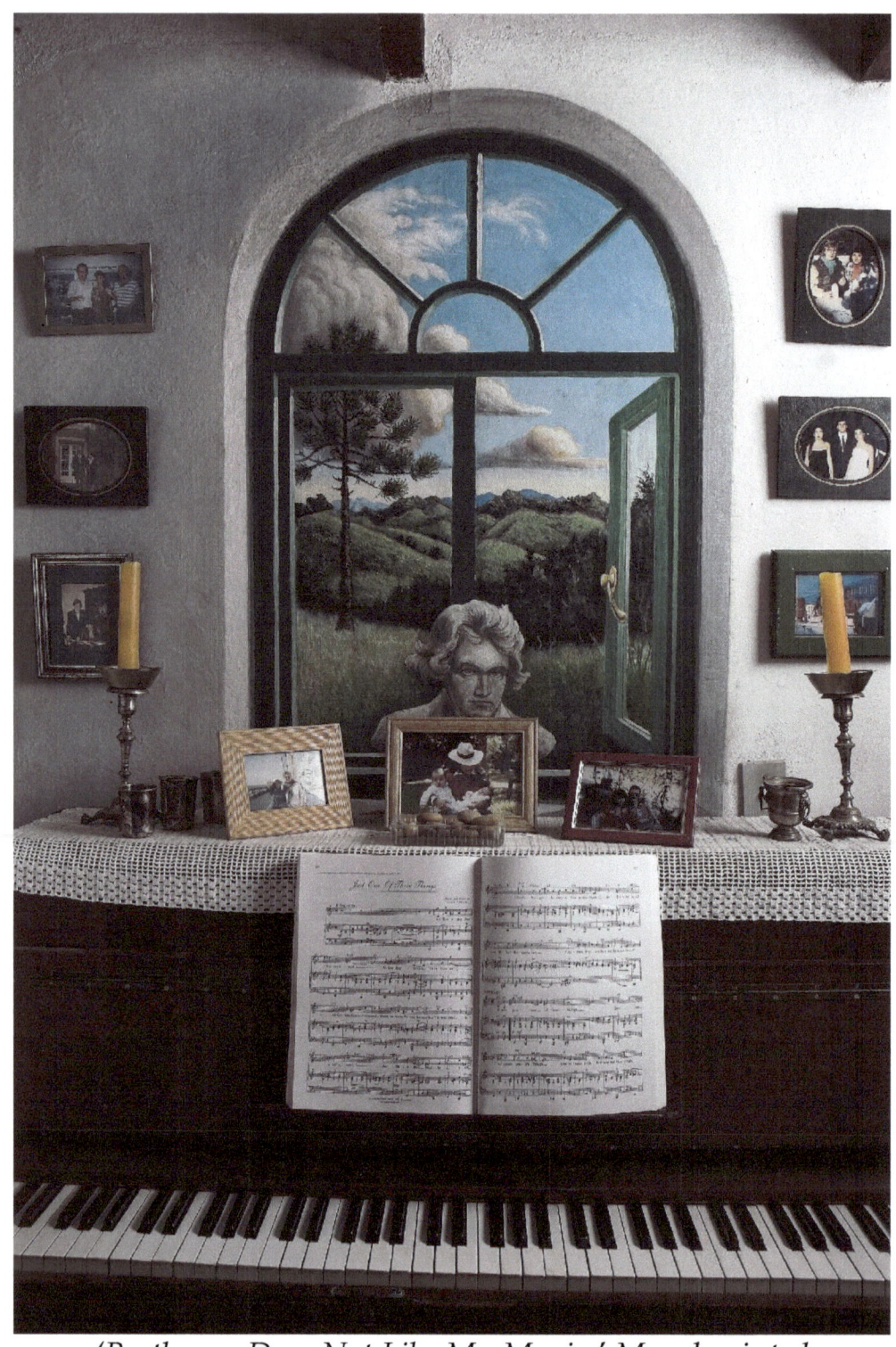

'Beethoven Does Not Like My Music.' Mural painted
at our house in Brazil.

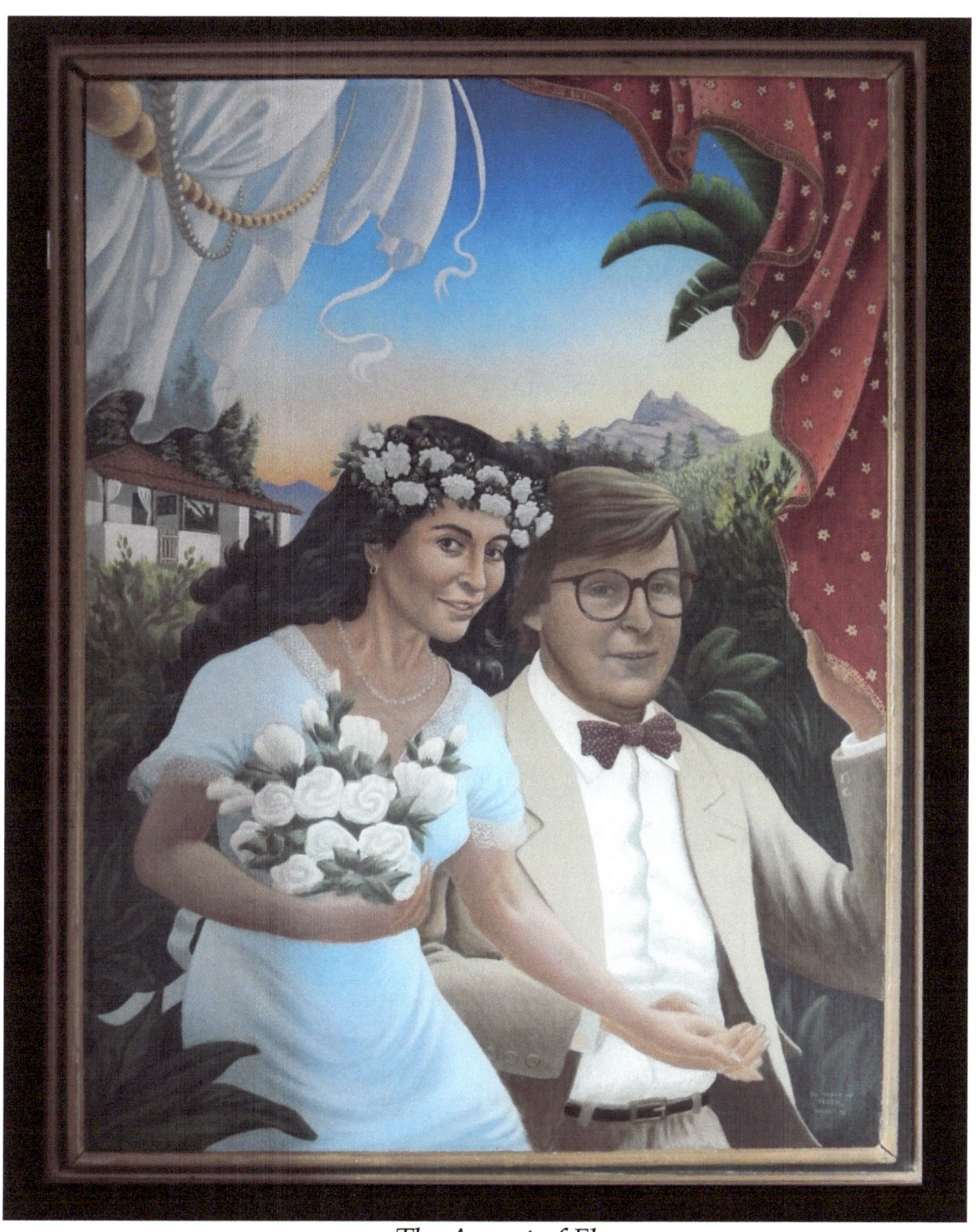

The Ascent of Flora

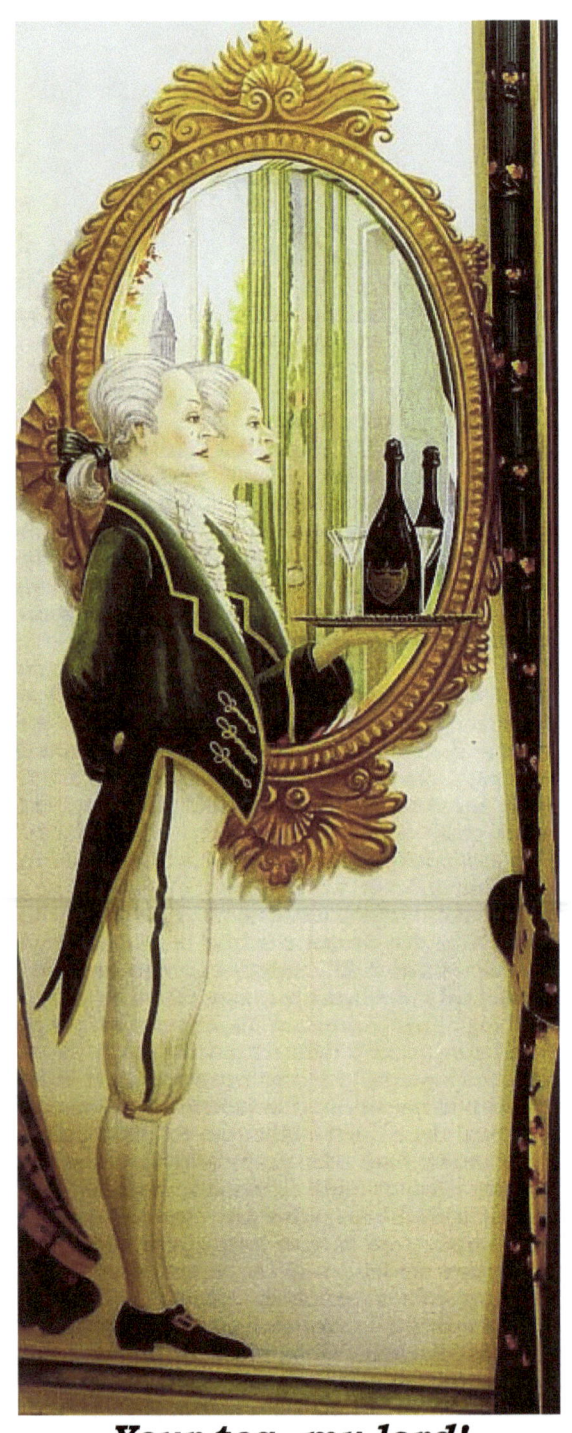

Your tea, my lord!
Composition in green and gold

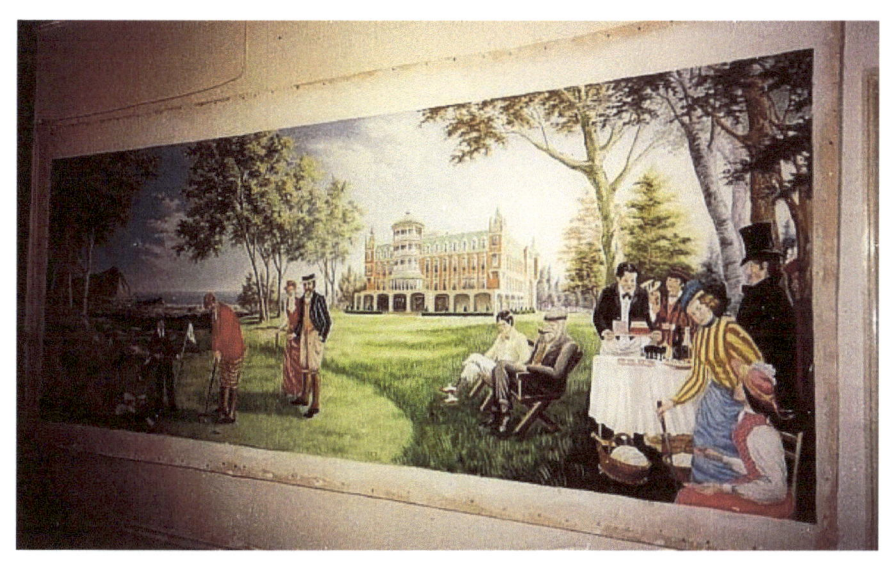

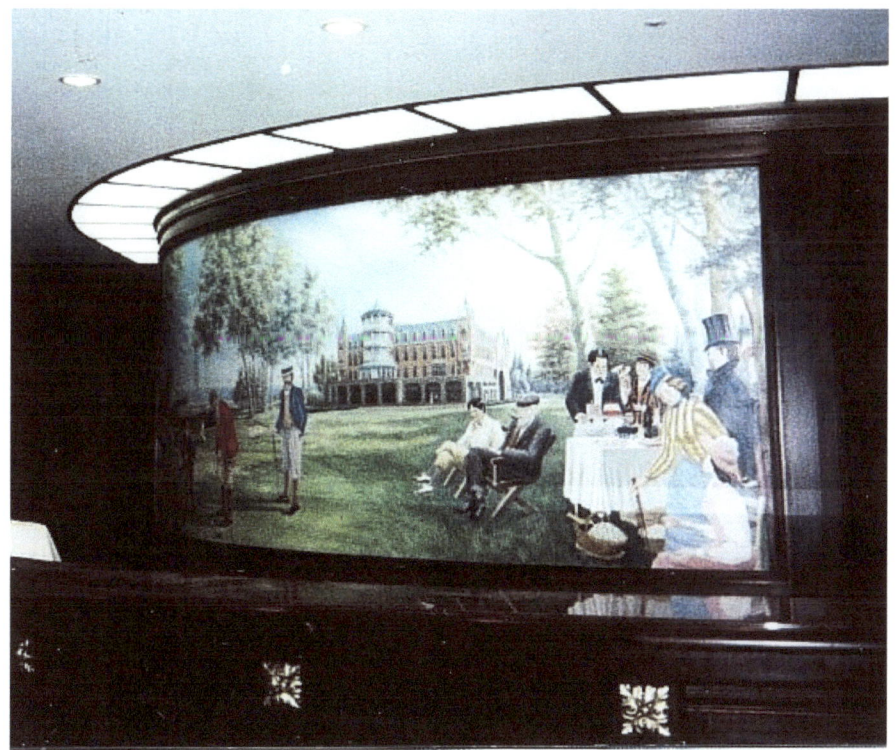

Concave mural of a period golfing scene, painted in London for the Yoishi Golf Club, Japan. 5x2.5m

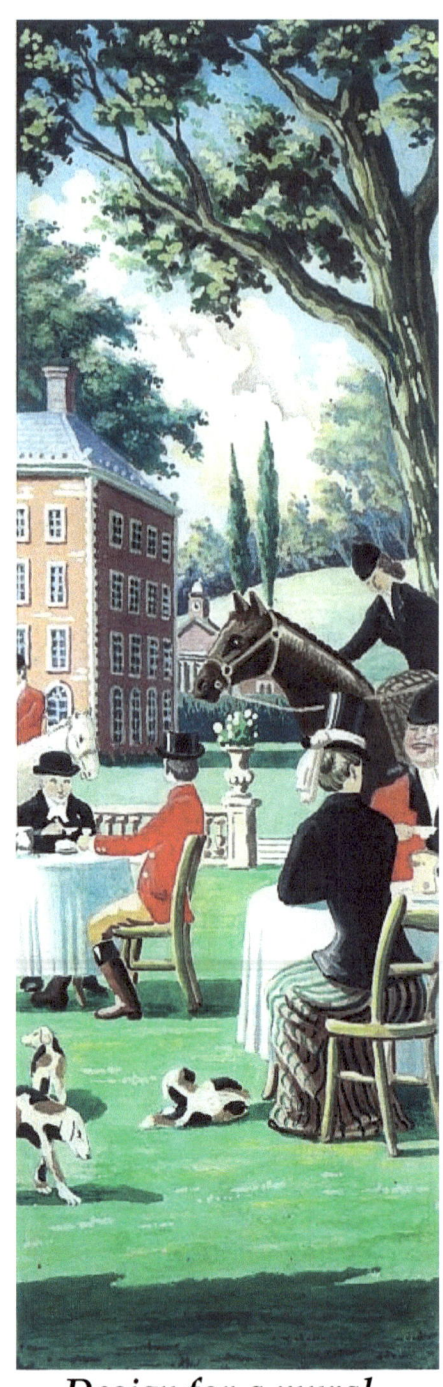

Design for a mural .
How very Right and Proper!

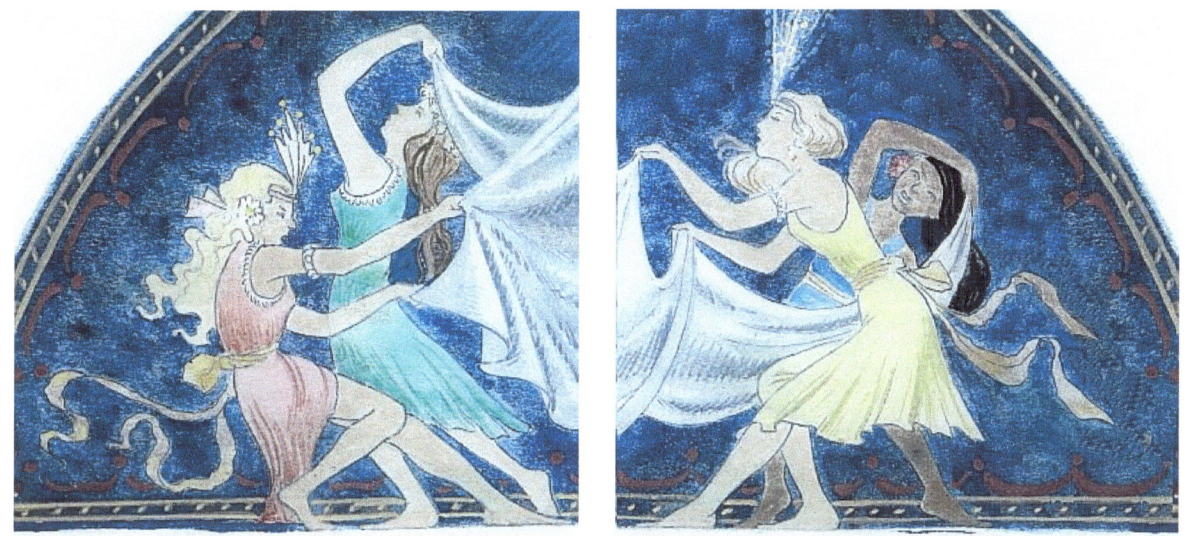

Designs for a mural – Figures erecting a screen

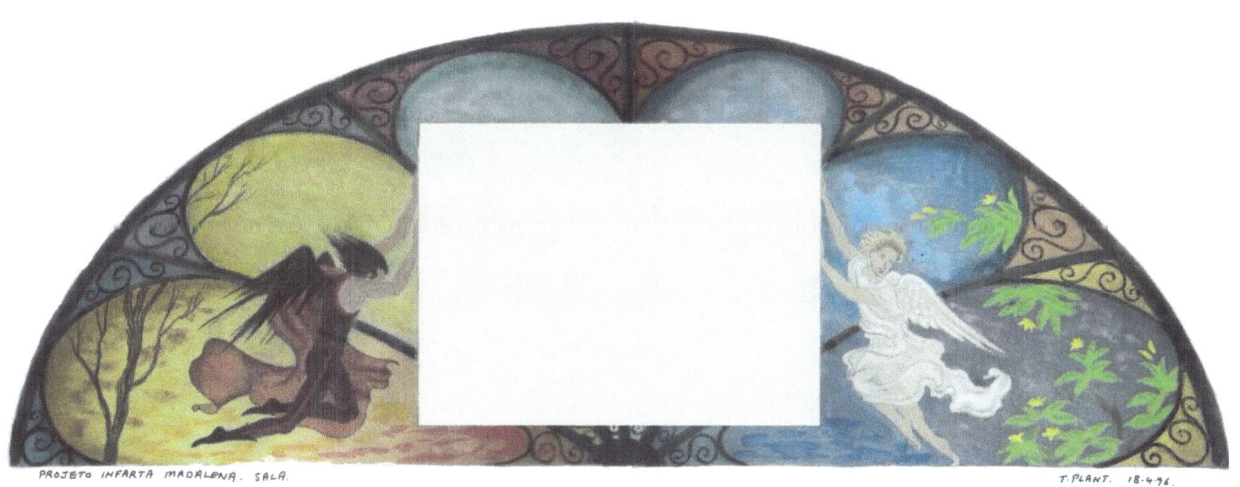

Figures supporting a screen

51

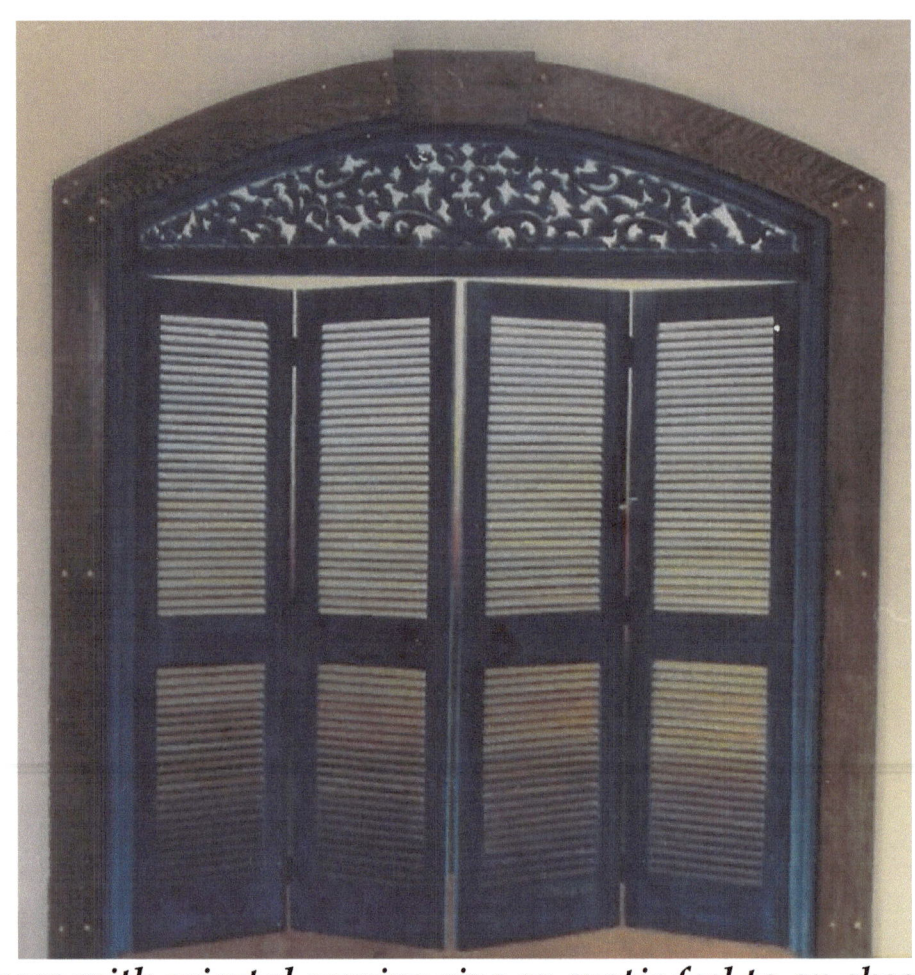

Louvre doors with oriental carving give an exotic feel to an absolutely flat wall, painted in the sports room of a villa close to London, England,.

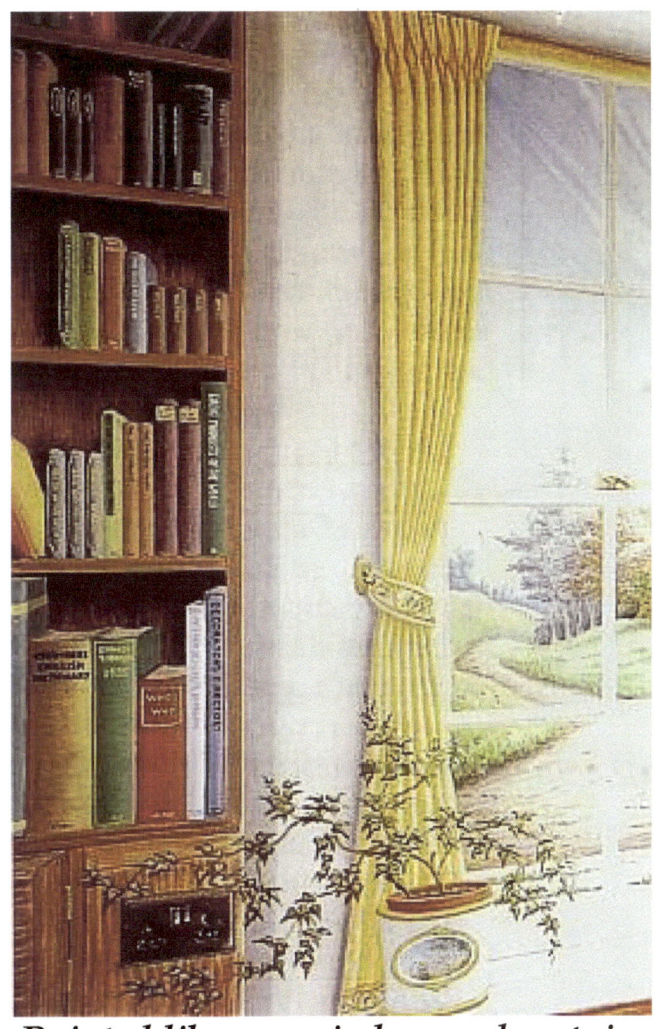

Painted library, window and curtains

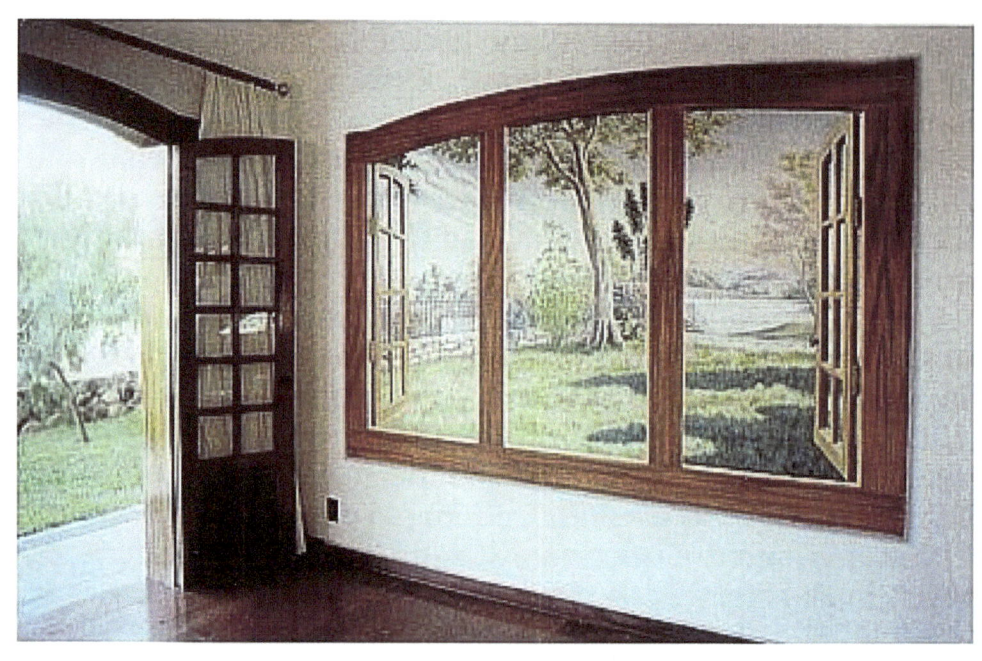

Painted window with continuation of garden.
Americana, SP, Brazil

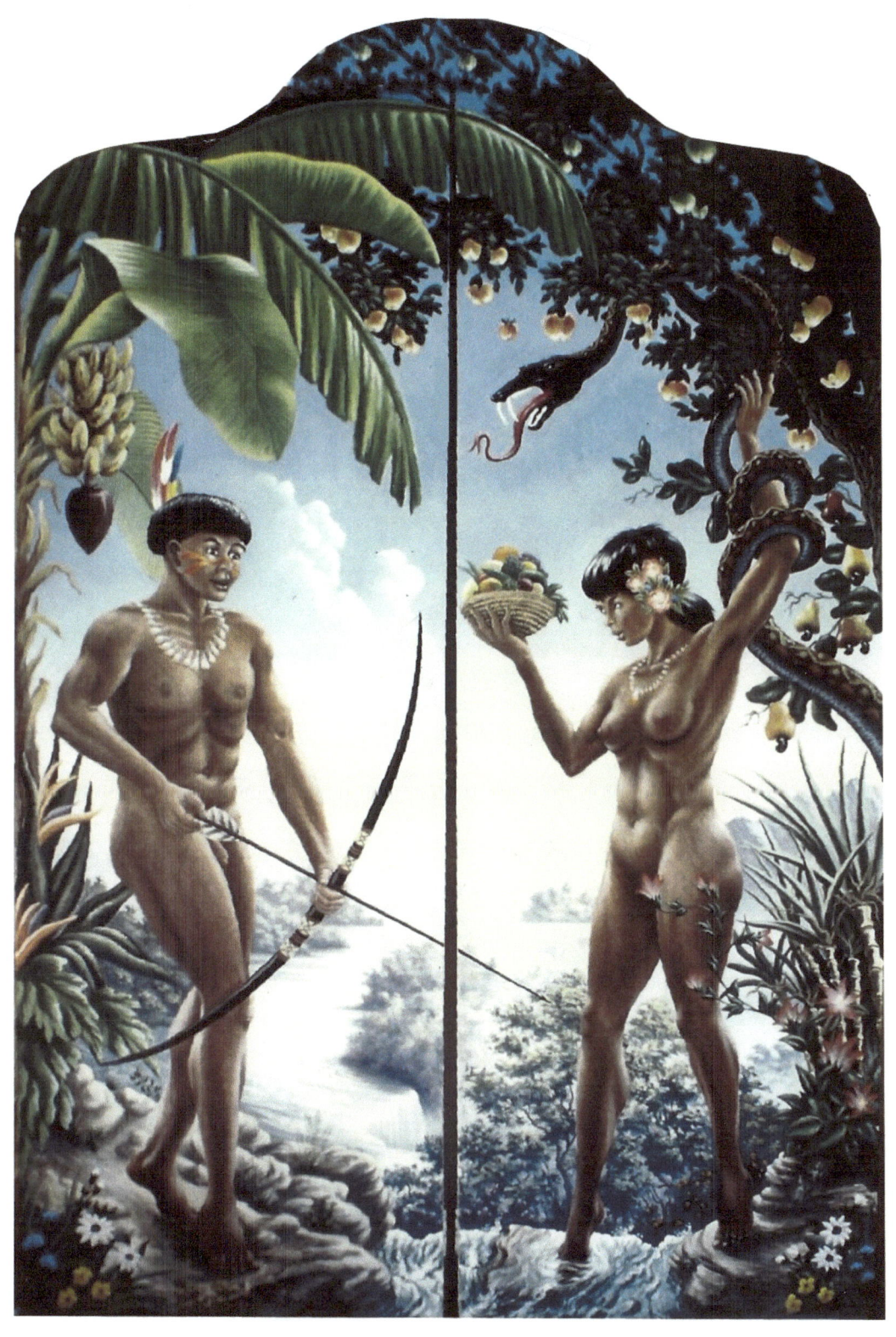

The Temptation of Eve – painted screen 2.5x1.75m

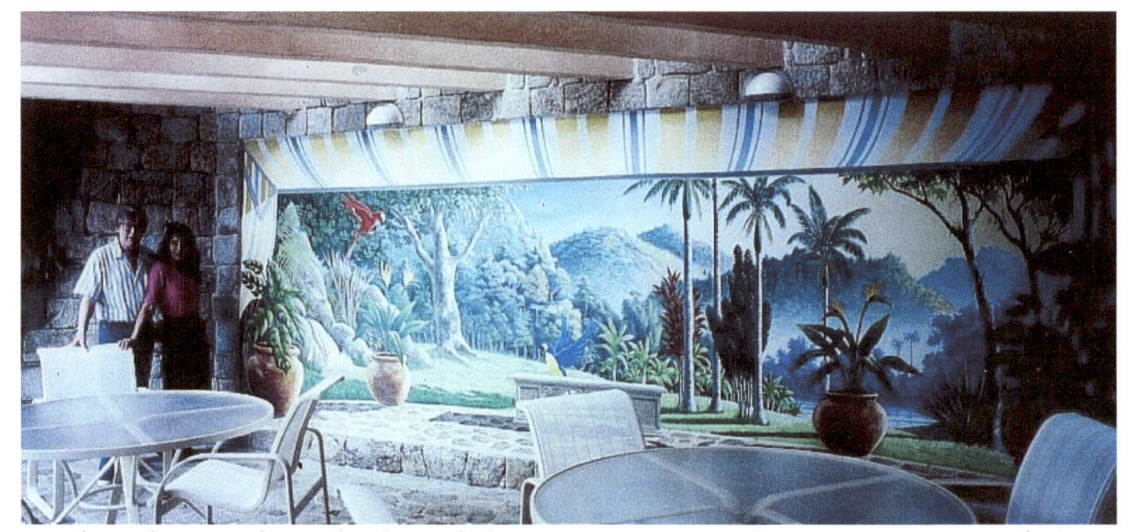

Completed mural at the beach house near Rio de Janeiro, Brazil, 8x2,5m

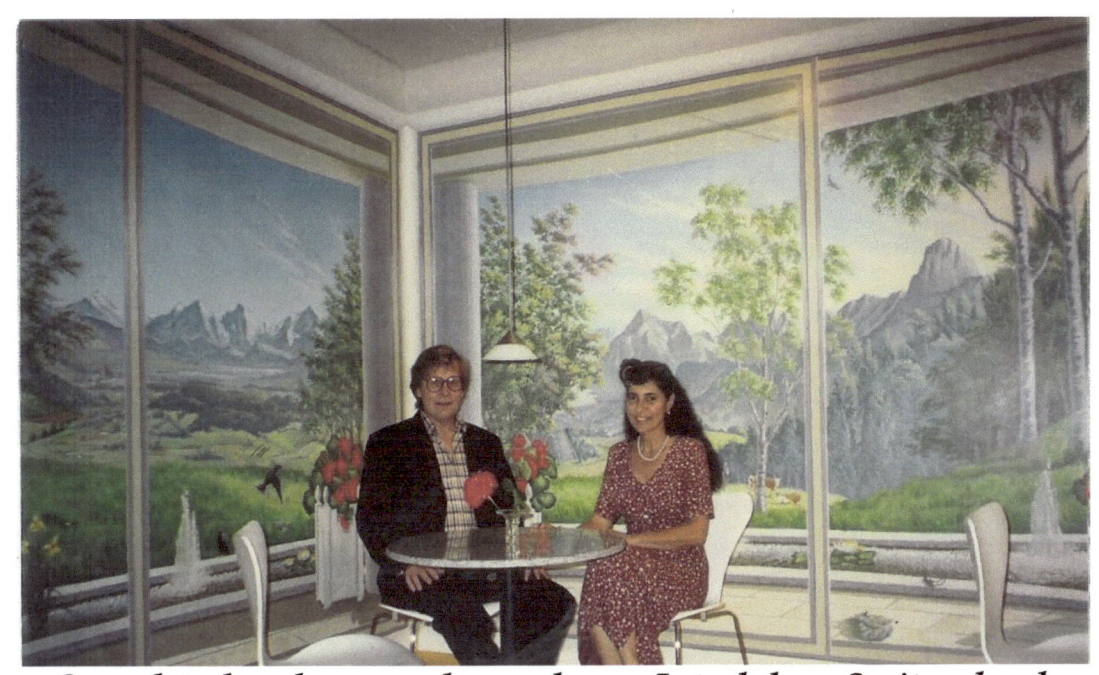

Completed underground mural near Interlaken, Switzerland.
10x3m

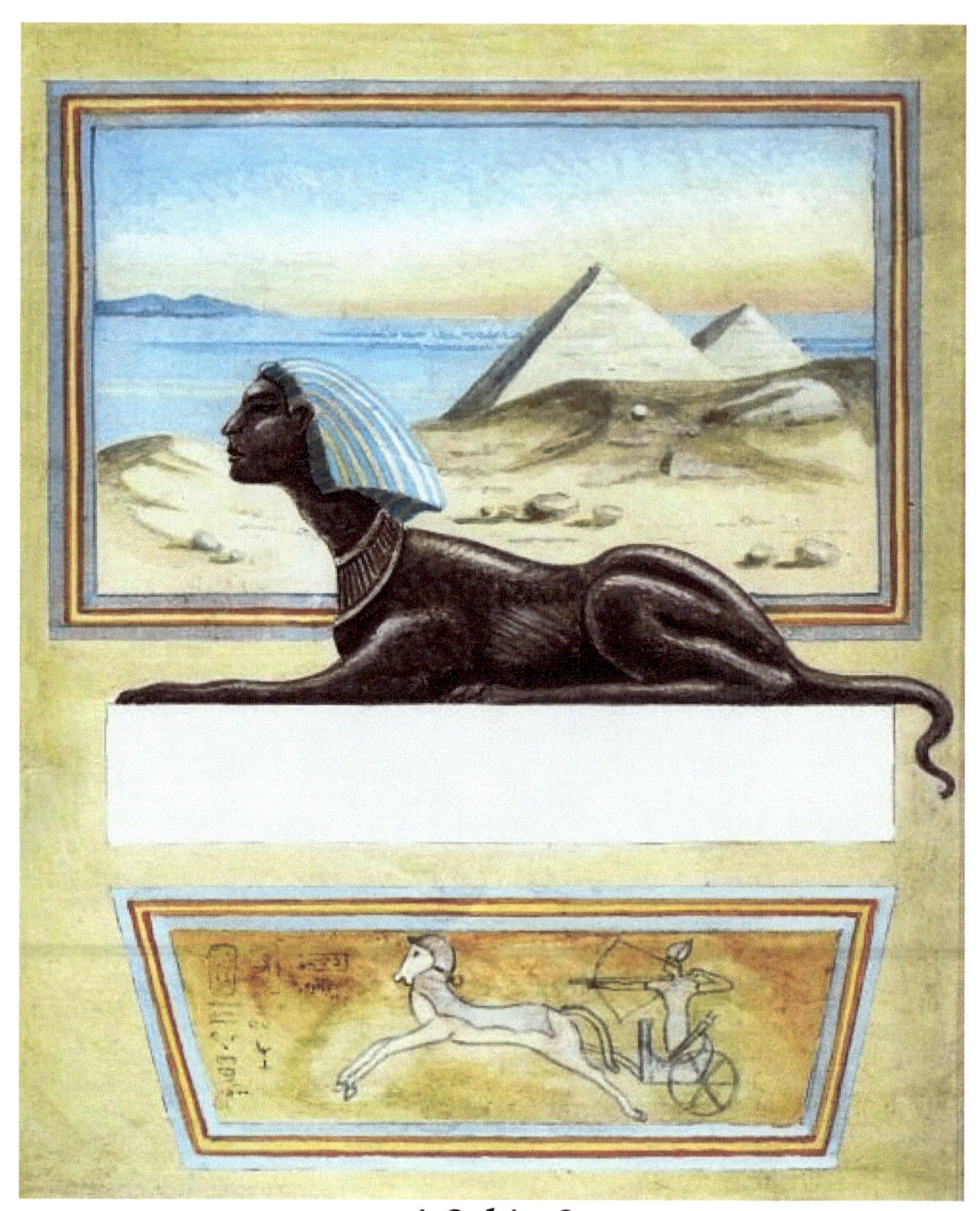

A Sphinx?

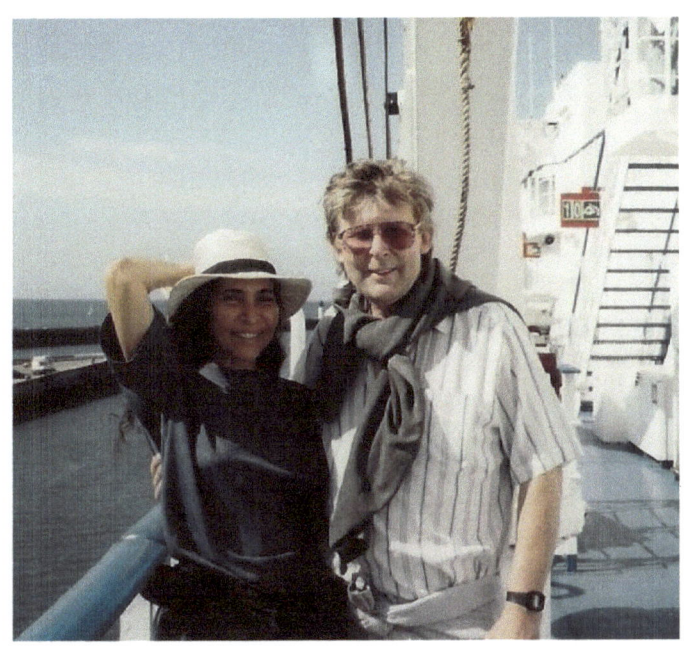

A Potted History of T. Plant

Timothy James Plant was born in Burton-upon-Trent, England, in 1943. He studied at St Edward's School, Oxford, and later at the University of Colorado, where he had his first literary experience in 1968, writing play revues for the Colorado Daily. He then went to Rome and spent five years painting pictures of the Eternal City, as well as interpreting and translating for a living. On his return to London at the age of 30 he continued his translating work, and painted on an amateur basis in the meantime. In 1978 he was commissioned to paint his first mural, an activity that took him to several countries, including Italy and Brazil. In 1987, Ward Lock of London commissioned him to write his first book, entitled PAINTED ILLUSIONS. This book was later published by Salem House in the USA. Volumes I & II of Timothy Plant's Trilogy 'Throw a Little Light' were published in the USA by Sterling House Inc. in 2006 and 2008. In 1993 he married the Brazilian artist Ana Maria Lampreia Carvalho. They spend most of their time between England and Brazil.

Other books by Timothy Plant

Painted Illusions
Beyond the Wall
The Microcosm
Watch It
Pibsterbule
The Phytanthrope
The Voyage of King Roy the First

www.ingramcontent.com/pod-product-compliance
Lightning Source LLC
Chambersburg PA
CBHW050804180526
45159CB00004B/1548